D1348742

Rational Theology and the Creativity of God

The real question is not whether we shall apply metaphysics; but whether our metaphysics is of the right kind

Hegel, *Logic*, 98

Rational Theology
and the Creativity of God

Keith Ward

Basil Blackwell · Oxford

© Keith Ward 1982

First published 1982
Basil Blackwell Publisher
108 Cowley Road
Oxford OX4 1JF
England

All rights reserved. No part of this publication may be reproduced, stored in a retrieval system, or transmitted, in any form or by any means, electronic, mechanical, photocopying, recording or otherwise, without the prior permission of Basil Blackwell Publisher Limited.

British Library Cataloguing in Publication Data

Ward, Keith
    Rational theology and the creativity of God
    1. God – Proof
    I. Title
    212'.1   BT102

    ISBN 0-631-12597-3

Typeset in 11 on 13pt IBM Journal by Freeman Graphic, Tonbridge

Printed and bound in Great Britain at
The Camelot Press Ltd, Southampton

Contents

This book is a slightly expanded and revised version of the Edward Cadbury Lectures, given in the University of Birmingham in 1980.

The Edward Cadbury Lectureship was established in 1941 by Edward Cadbury Esquire, LL.D. for the furtherance of the study of Theology in the University of Birmingham. According to the Regulations there shall be an annual course of Lectures, usually eight in number, to be delivered in either the Autumn or Spring Term. The theme of the Lectures shall be concerned with some aspect of the Christian faith, the original intention of the Founder being that it should be concerned with the relations past, present and future, of Christianity to civilization and culture.

1   The Intelligibility of Being

My intention in this book is to develop and defend a notion of God which is internally consistent, coherent with our other knowledge of the universe, and compatible with the beliefs of the major theistic religions. I shall also try to show that there are good reasons for asserting the existence of such a being, and that most of the great classical philosophers have not been wrong when they have held that the existence of God is the foundation of all being and value, and that belief in God is the highest expression of human rationality, and the guardian of our commitment to the ultimate value of human life and endeavour.

These two tasks — of expounding the idea of God, and of establishing the rationality and moral importance of belief in God — go together. Without a clear idea of God, one cannot be sure of what, exactly, one is looking for reasons to accept. And without a clear account of the reasons for belief, one cannot be sure of what it is that one has established as the conclusion of those reasonings. In the history of rational theology, there have been a number of different ideas of God, similar in some respects but importantly different in others. I shall argue, and try to show, that two contrasting models of God have dominated the history of philosophical theology, both in the Indian and European traditions. I shall not say much about the Indian tradition, though I shall point to parallels with European philosophy from time to time. The two models I have in mind may be distinguished by their differing interpretations of the idea of 'infinity'. Both agree in defining God as an infinite, eternal and self-existent being, from which the universe takes its origin and upon which the universe depends for its existence at all times. They also agree in regarding God as perfect in a sense that no finite being can match, as a being than which no greater or more perfect can be conceived. And they agree that God exists necessarily and is the ground of all the rational necessities which make the universe intelligible. All these claims are contentious; but I think they can all be retained and defended. I shall attempt to do so, and will thus be defending what could be called the traditional philosophical idea of God, in its essential elements.

But this traditional idea, as I have mentioned, has been interpreted in two rather different ways. In one tradition, which may be termed the tradition of 'inclusive infinity', God has been understood as including all possible and actual things within himself. One might mention Plotinus, Ramanuja, Spinoza, Hegel and Whitehead as belonging to this tradition. The whole universe is an expression, or emanation, of the unlimited reality of God, or the Absolute; he includes it within his being, though he is not limited by its finite forms. The other tradition may be called the tradition of 'exclusive infinity'; in being infinite, God excludes all finite things from himself. He is fully real in himself alone; no addition of finite realities to him can really be an addition, since he is already infinite; so the world is neither necessary to God, nor does it make any difference to his unlimited reality. The most influential exponent of this tradition is Aquinas, though Descartes, Leibniz and Kant, together with most Christian theologians, also belong to it. For this reason, it is often identified with traditional Christian theism, though it must be pointed out that both Hegel and Whitehead have their followers, usually among Protestant theologians.

My central argument will be that neither tradition is capable of dealing adequately with a crucial difficulty which arises when the relation of God, the necessary, eternal, perfect and immutable being, to a universe of contingent, and even free, beings is considered. The difficulty, put briefly, is this: if our demand for the rational intelligibility of the universe is to be satisfied, God must be a necessary, eternal and therefore changeless, individual. But if our demand for human freedom and the contingency of the finite world is to be met, and especially if we wish to speak of free creation, either by God or human beings, then it cannot be the case that the universe depends solely upon a necessary being. For the truly contingent cannot arise from the wholly necessary; and, if creation, Divine or human, is free and contingent, then creation is incompatible with necessity. If God is the creator or cause of a contingent world, he must be contingent and temporal; but if God is a necessary being, then whatever he causes must be necessary and changelessly caused. On this rock both traditional interpretations of theism founder. The demands of intelligibility require the existence of a necessary, immutable, eternal being. Creation seems to demand a contingent, temporal God, who interacts with creation and is, therefore, not self-sufficient. But how can one have both?

I shall argue that both traditional interpretations must be rejected. But this requires, not a rejection of the traditional idea of God, but a revision of it, utilizing an idea of infinity which may be called that of 'dynamic infinity', a move which requires the admission of potency and temporality in God, but which can be reconciled with a properly interpreted doctrine of eternity and necessity. So it is possible and proper to think of God as a necessary, eternal and infinite being, who is the free creator of everything other than himself. God is the one self-existent being in whom creation and necessity originate and in whom they are reconciled.

That is the conclusion towards which I am moving. But the first question to ask is how one gets to the notion of a necessary being in the first place. It is a very sophisticated idea; it is not found, for example, anywhere in the Bible. It is, one might say, a philosopher's idea rather than a believer's idea. But I suppose it is none the worse for that. So let us examine it on its merits. We can return later to the question of how it relates to religious notions of God, though I hope it is clear that I regard it as quite compatible with them and indeed a necessary complement to them. The genesis of this notion of God, then, lies in the attempt to say what things must be like if the demand for the rational intelligibility of the world is to be satisfied. As one reflects upon the nature of the world, one seeks general rational principles which can explain why it is as it is. This search for general explanation is a deep-rooted propensity of the human mind; man, as a rational being, is by nature oriented towards a quest for intelligibility. The search may be successful or not; but the orientation itself is not inferred from any other basic principle. The supposition that rational explanations for occurrences do exist and can be found is not a supposition that can be justified inductively from experience. We have to presuppose it, to get any explanations in the first place. It has the status of an ultimate postulate or conjecture, though of course repeated success in discovering explanations will increase our confidence in it. It assumes that the universe is grounded upon an intelligible, explanatory order, upon the necessity and immutability of basic natural processes. This is a conjecture which Karl Popper terms 'metaphysical', in that it is not subject to falsification by a test-case, but which he thinks is both true and important (*The Logic of Scientific Discovery*, p. 438). The strength of this assumption even for a scientist who is not at all interested in theological matters can be found expressed in a revealing sentence from Steven Weinberg's *The First Three Minutes,* a popular account of recent cosmological hypotheses. After stating the cosmological theory that the initial state of this universe requires a 1000:1 ratio of photons to nuclear particles, he bemoans the fact that explanation may have to stop at this ultimate point; for, he says, 'We would prefer a greater sense of logical inevitability in the theory' (p. 17). The ideal of scientific understanding is to have one extremely simple and logically inevitable theory. This may be an impossible request where scientific explanation is concerned; for, if physical explanations are in terms of general laws and initial conditions, how could those ultimate laws and conditions be explained physically? Yet the quest for fuller explanation is still there, pushing beyond the physical to what Weinberg calls the 'logically inevitable'. What the theist basically argues is that this assumption, or pre-orientation of the mind to assume that reality is rational can only be adequately substantiated if there exists one self-explanatory being which explains all others.

The traditional cosmological proofs of God can be interpreted as explorations of the idea of the intelligibility of the world. They cannot get started without the basic assumption that there is a complete explanation for the world. One can always, like Hume, say that no such explanation is necessary or possible, and therefore simply accept a coming into being from nothing or an infinite series of caused causes. All the proofs of God can do is to spell out what is involved in the claim that the world is fully intelligible, and attempt to establish the possibility of such perfect intelligibility. In them, the mind both seeks to clarify the methods of its own rational operation and to ask what sort of object would fully satisfy those demands.

One could never establish beyond doubt the reality of such a wholly intelligible object without being able to discern reality as one intelligible totality, which is beyond human capacity. The most one can do is to show the coherence of such an object, to draw consequences from its posited existence and to ask whether these seem to square with the world of one's experience. So the question from which one must begin is this: what would it be like for the world to be fully intelligible?

A quest for intelligibility breaks down if we cannot answer the question, 'Why does this exist, with the nature it has?' One natural and primitive way of answering that question is to refer to some purpose: 'It exists because I want it to'. Thus the weather might be accounted for by the purposive activities of Zeus. But one can then push the question further and ask, 'Why do you have those desires?' Then the answer will probably be given in terms of general laws governing the emergence of new things and properties and of initial states over which the laws range. But why are those laws and states as they are? One might derive them from some more general laws and prior states, but, in the end, one must arrive at some basic law or laws of nature and some first initial state. Can one push the 'why' even further back? Or is one bound to end with some statement of brute fact eventually?

If intelligibility comes to an end somewhere, one cannot be sure that it does not come to an end with ultimate laws of physics. Reference to a God would only defer the arbitrary stopping place and give no special intellectual advantage — unless there is a further stage, not yet touched upon. That would have to be a stage at which the description of what exists does not raise the question, 'Why is it thus?' Its simple description would have to provide the reason for its being as it is. Can one conceive such a reality? One would have to conceive of a being whose sheer nature explains its existence, as well as the existence of everything else. Seeing what it is, one would see that it must be as it is and could not be otherwise. It would have to be a self-explanatory being.

Many modern philosophers think that the idea of such a being is incoherent or vacuous. Professor Swinburne, in *The Existence of God,* distinguishes various sorts of explanation to which a theist might appeal. He terms a 'complete explanation' one in which initial conditions plus either a natural law or an intention, belief and capacity necessitate the item to be explained, and in which there is no further explanation of those factors in terms of other factors operative at the same time. Thus appeal to the existence of a God plus a reference to his intentions and abilities might necessitate the existence of a universe like this one. God's present intentions might in turn be explicable in terms of previous acts and intentions of his, even though there are no other present factors which could explain them. God would then provide a complete explanation of the existence of the universe now.

An 'ultimate explanation' he defines as a complete explanation which has the additional feature that the ultimate terms of the explanation cannot themselves be explained at all, either in the present or in the past. They are, he says, 'ultimate brute facts'. If God necessarily exists at all times, he says, then any complete explanation in terms of God's action at a certain time would also be an ultimate explanation (*The Existence of God,* p. 77). I do not think this is quite right, for God's present intention may be in part explicable by some past act or intention of his. For example, his intention to make David King of Israel was in part due to his prior decision to reject the dynasty of Saul. If God is, as Swinburne thinks, everlasting, this means that he can only provide a complete, never an ultimate explanation; for each present act of God will depend upon an infinite number of past intentions or acts. However, in either case, explanation will end with certain brute facts, incapable of any further explanation. Yet in this respect, God differs from the universe, which is capable of further explanation (in terms of God's purpose), whether or not it has such an explanation.

Swinburne distinguishes one further form of explanation, which he calls 'absolute explanation'. Here, the basic factors would not be merely incapable of further explanation; they would be self-explanatory or logically necessary. I think it is clear that this would be a more complete form of explanation, which left literally nothing unexplained, and it is the sort of explanation I have in mind. But Swinburne gives two reasons why he does not believe there can be absolute explanations. First, he says, nothing can explain itself: that is, the idea of a self-explanatory being is incoherent or vacuous. Second, the logically necessary cannot explain the logically contingent: anything entailed by the necessary must itself be necessary, so a logically necessary being could not explain a contingent world at all. When I wrote *The Concept of God,* I was inclined to agree (pp. 138–52), and stressed, in addition, that the incomprehensible, as God is usually said to be, could not explain the merely mysterious. But I have now revised my opinion.

It is true that we cannot comprehend any being the sheer possibility of which necessitates, and thus explains, its actual existence and the existence of whatever depends upon it. But the idea of such a being is not, so far as we can see, self-contradictory; and I believe that enough can be said about the properties it must possess for it to be a non-vacuous idea. That is what I intend to do now. As for the necessary not entailing the contingent, that is, of course, quite correct. It is, indeed, a particular form of the crucial difficulty about the relation of creation to necessity with which I am centrally concerned. It clearly requires making God, the self-explanatory being, contingent in some respects. I shall explore this notion in detail later, but I will say now that I think Swinburne's mistake, and that of most other theists who have discussed the issue, is to insist that God is either necessary in all respects, or contingent in all respects — just the ultimate contingent fact. Whereas, as I shall argue, we can have both necessity and contingency in God. And we need both. As for the point about the incomprehensible not explaining the mysterious, all that need be said is that God is not incomprehensible to himself; being self-explanatory, after all, does not entail that anyone else can understand the explanation, only that it exists.

So I do think that the notion of a self-explanatory being is coherent, is the most complete possible form of explanation and is the only adequate foundation of the intelligibility of the universe. I do not agree, either, with Professor Hick, who holds that 'we can accept the existence of purposive intelligence as an ultimate fact' (*Arguments for the Existence of God,* p. 50), for, 'to us . . . the fact of conscious mental existence is not a candidate for explanation'. This seems to me to be an appeal to anthropomorphic prejudice, and not at all to catch the force of 'self-explanation'. I am a mind, but I still think that the nature and existence of minds requires further explanation. In fact, I rather agree with Hume that minds are more complex than matter, and so require more, not less, explanation. Even if, as Hick claims, we cannot conceive of another reality in terms of which mind might be explained, this does not give mind an explanatory ultimacy. We are still left with all the problems of why this mind is as it is, and of how it is that it can be self-existent, and of how it can produce matter, if it does. In other words, I think that the existence of a contingent but wholly independent cosmic mind is the paradigm of mystery, not of explanation at all. It may be that is all we can have. But if that mind just happens to exist and to explain the universe, if that is an ultimate contingent fact about the world, then it seems that there might well have been a universe, very like this one, but without God; or, even more worrying perhaps, that there might have been a being very like God, who created the world yet was not good or eternal.

Those who hold that the existence of God is contingent do seem to be committed to such possibilities. It can only be good fortune that their search for an ultimate or complete explanation is successful. Whereas I wish to maintain that, even if we cannot prove that there is an absolute explanation of the world, if there is one, then there necessarily is one; there cannot fail to be one. Subjectively, I postulate an absolute explanation, but objectively, if I am right, the existence of such explanation is necessary in every possible world. There could not be a world without God, and there could not be a being very like, but not quite like, God in place of the God there is. I think that such claims as these are meaningful — which in itself shows that the idea of a self-explanatory being is not vacuous — and are required as conditions of the intelligibility of the world. For the world is not truly intelligible if it could have been otherwise; the limits of the intelligible, as Swinburne sees, are the limits of rational necessity.

What I want to do now is to see what can be said of a self-explanatory being, and thus to show that its notion has content. It is clear that, if any being is to be self-explanatory, it must be existentially self-sufficient; that is, it can depend upon nothing other than itself for its existence. For if it did depend upon something else for its existence, one could not wholly explain why it was as it was, including why it existed at all, without reference to that other thing; so it would not, after all, be self-explanatory. Now if it depends upon nothing else for its existence, it certainly cannot depend upon itself for its existence; that is, it cannot bring itself into being, for it would first have to exist to be able to bring itself into existence, which is self-contradictory. Thus its existence can depend upon nothing, neither upon itself nor some other being. It must, therefore, always have existed; it must be uncaused, either by itself or by another. The only alternative is that it comes into being from nothing, but that would entail that it could not be completely explained. For there would be no reason at all why it should have come into being or have the nature that it has. Something essentially unexplained, indeed inexplicable, would always remain; which contradicts the hypothesis that this is a self-explanatory being.

It may be thought that the self-explanatory being could be a complex reality, within which A explains another part, B, and B in turn explains A. But that is not possible. For each element would need its existence explained by reference to some other element, and such explanation could not be symmetrical. If one explains why B comes into being by referring to A, which already exists and brings it into being, then one cannot in the same way explain why A comes into being by referring to B, since B will not exist at that time. So the parts of a self-explanatory being cannot be mutually explanatory; at least some of them must be wholly uncaused. An infinite regress of causes is ruled out, for then everything would have to be explained by reference to something else, so that the explanation could never be complete.

The conclusion remains that there must be one or more uncaused causes, as a condition of the total intelligibility of the world. These do not just happen to be uncaused and thus everlasting, as though they might have had a cause, but did not. For to say that they could have had a cause is to say that they could have been brought into being, or might not have been; then they are no longer self-explanatory, for there will have to be something else which explains why they are. The uncaused cause (or causes) is logically *a se*; its existence and nature is derived from itself alone — not by causal derivation, but by logical derivation.

This is essentially the argument Aquinas gives in the *secunda via* (*Summa Theologiae,* qu. 2, art. 3). He says that nothing can bring itself into being; efficient causality is irreflexive. But the series of causes must stop, or no effects would begin to be. He does not elaborate a further argument for excluding an infinite regress of causes. But, as has been seen, such an argument may appeal to the impossibility of a complete explanation without some uncaused cause. However, an infinite temporal regress may be, as Aquinas says elsewhere (qu. 46, art. 2) possible in principle. In fact, Aquinas seems to speak of a series of simultaneously active efficient causes, rather than of a temporally regressive series. It is difficult to see that such a series is possible, or what it is. But one may hold that the uncaused cause is not part of the temporal series, but is eternal, in the sense of timeless. The temporal series as a whole depends upon it, and thus may be without beginning or end, though it is timelessly generated by the first cause.

Many of the popular refutations of this argument rest on a misunderstanding of what it is trying to do. The most popular, and most mistaken, is that it begins from the axiom that every event must have a cause, which it then simply contradicts by supposing a first event, God, which has no cause.

Aquinas was not that stupid, however. The premiss is that everything that comes into being has a cause; then it is asserted that there cannot be an infinite regress of causes, because if there were, the search for a total explanation would be doomed. So there must be a being which does not come into being, and this requires, and can have, no cause. It is not a proof which will convince anyone, whatever his state of mind — as though 'God' could suddenly pop up in the conclusion of a syllogism, when he was nowhere in the premisses. The medievals' grasp of logic was too refined to suppose that such a process of proof was possible. Rather, it is an analysis of the notion of complete explanation, and what is implied in the thought of its possibility. It commits one to the existence of God only if one accepts the intelligibility of the universe. There is no way to force a man to do that; it is an ultimate assumption which will appeal, if it does, by its coherence as a focal point of many related strands of argument to do with the importance of personal being, the objectivity of value, the appropriateness of prayer and the preconditions of the pursuit of science.

Aquinas's *prima via* may similarly be reconstructed as seeking to establish that there must exist something unchanged: not only not brought into being, but also not modified or affected in any way, either by itself or by another. He argues that all changing things are changed by something else. His argument is that change is a passing from having x potentially to having x actually; change must be caused by something actual, something which already has x actually. We might well not agree with this axiom that causes must possess the properties they are to bring about in their effects, though it was fairly universally accepted in early and medieval philosophy. But we might agree that a change must be caused by some logically prior state, either in that object or in some other, if explanation is to be possible (if there is to be some reason for x rather than y). Thomas next excludes an infinite regress, and therefore arrives at some state which is unchanged, since there can be nothing prior to it to change it. We might again agree that, if there is to be a complete explanation for *x*, there cannot be an infinite regress of changes. There must be an end to the giving of reasons, which will lie in some self-explanatory state. In the *secunda via*, the main point to be established was that the first cause must be uncaused, not brought into being, underived, without beginning and self-sufficient. The main point of the *prima via* is to establish that the first cause of all change cannot be changed at all, even by itself. So it can never change or cease to be; it is immutable and imperishable.

The principle of the argument is exactly the same in the two ways. Change is, after all, a form of causality. So to admit that A was changed by B would be to deny A's self-explanatoriness. To say that A can change itself is to embark on an infinite series of causes within A, unless one comes to a first state, cause of all subsequent changes but itself unchanged. This argument enables one to establish that there can only be one prime mover, or unchanged changer (it is important to see that the argument is not simply from the fact of motion or movement, but from any change of state whatsoever). Suppose there were two. Each would be immutable, underived and imperishable (if they cannot change, they obviously cannot cease to exist). So neither could affect the other in any way. Each explains, not only itself, but also everything caused by it. So none of their effects could *relate* causally to effects in the other set, since that would impugn their explanatory role. Therefore there can be only one prime mover for each self-contained explicable universe of causally related items. It is thus true that in such a universe there can be only one immutable first cause.

But could this universe not contain diverse sets of explanatory items, not causally related, each tracing back to an immutable cause? One has to bear in mind that, on the theory, each such cause will be self-existent. That is, it will depend upon nothing other than itself for its existence and nature; and it will exist in every possible world, since there is no possible world which could cause it not to exist, and its existence follows simply from its own nature — that is what self-explanatoriness means. So we are asked to conceive of many totally independent beings, which are yet such that, if one exists, all exist (for, if each must exist in every possible world, none can exist without the others). But it is contradictory to say both that x is totally self-explanatory, requiring reference to nothing other than itself to account for its existence, and that x cannot exist without y, which cannot in turn be explained by reference to x (since it, too, is self-explanatory). Since x and y exist in all possible worlds, x cannot exist without y; therefore x cannot completely account for its own existence, which must logically depend on the existence of y, which x itself does not explain. This is just a spelling-out of what it means to say that a being is wholly self-explanatory — it must not depend on any other being in any way for its existence or nature. It follows that, as a matter of logic, there can only be one self-explanatory being.

Nevertheless, may this first cause not have been different from what it is? Aquinas's *tertia via* begins from the consideration that some things need not be what they are; they are contingent. He argues that in an infinite time every possibility will be realized, including the possibility that all contingent beings will pass out of existence at the same time. This is in fact false, since in an infinite time a finite set of possibilities could keep recurring, while some possibilities never occurred at all. But it is certainly *possible* that, if everything was contingent, everything could cease to exist at once. And perhaps the fact that this possibility could occur is enough to worry Thomas. For if it did occur, then there would exist nothing; and, he says, nothing comes from nothing. So, he concludes, since there is something (neglecting the consideration that an infinite time may not yet have elapsed), not everything can be contingent. There must be at least one necessary being, incapable of coming to be and passing away.

Certainly, it seems that, if there is no necessary being, the world may cease to exist at any moment. True, we assume that it will not, because the basic laws of physics will continue to operate. Of course, they themselves, any or all of them, could cease at any moment. One may hold that there are natural necessities, in that, given a physical law z, then events a, b . . . will necessarily occur. That is so; yet, if the law x is itself contingent, events a, b . . . cannot really be necessary, since they could change at any time if x changed. Necessities which are grounded on some ultimately contingent fact are not truly necessary at all; they are contingent on that fact being the case. But can there be an ultimate necessity, not conditional on some further given fact? If so, it would have to be something which could not fail to be, and to be what it is. It seems to me that if there is not such a being, then there cannot ultimately be coherence and intelligibility in the world, except as an amazing freak of chance. For at every moment the basic laws of nature could simply cease to be, and there is nothing which, as it were, compels them to remain in being; so the longer they stay in existence the more unlikely it seems that they will continue to do so. Naturally, one cannot prove that they do not just happen to continue. That fact would give rise to wonder, though not religious wonder; rather, a shuddering fear in the face of the abyss which continually confronts nature as a possibility. Religious wonder is different in quality; it too experiences awe in face of the regularity of nature, but it sees in that regularity a ground of necessary intelligibility which transcends human reason and inspires a sense of absolute dependence and ultimate hope.

But we have already arrived at the postulate of an uncaused and imperishable being; is this all the 'Third Way' seeks to establish? Many commentators have argued that it is; by a necessary being Thomas means only one which exists for ever, which does not have the potentiality for coming to be or passing away. Geach and Anscombe are adamant that Aquinas did not mean by Divine necessity the logical necessity of a proposition to the effect that 'God exists' (even if Leibniz did mean that). Divine necessity is, they say, 'imperishable existence that has no liability to cease' (*Three Philosophers,* p. 115). So, spirits and human souls (for Aquinas) have no 'inherent liability to stop existing'; they cannot change or decompose. But God is imperishable 'underivatively or in its own right'. Of course, any immutable or timeless being is imperishable; so, in saying that God exists necessarily, Aquinas is saying that he is both independent of any other being, causally, and immutable and eternal (if he ever exists, he cannot then change or cease to be). Such a conception would ensure that the laws of nature could not just cease to operate at any moment, whatever God willed in the matter. For, even if God is contingent, if he exists at all, he always (or eternally) does; we are delivered from the worry that things might just cease to be or change radically for no reason. Is that not enough, without requiring, further, that God could not have failed to be?

The view that it is enough has found wide support. Swinburne, in *The Coherence of Theism,* carefully distinguishes six different senses in which a proposition may be said to be necessary. His conclusion is that the proposition 'God exists' is necessary in the sense that what it states is never dependent on anything other than itself, or what it entails. Its truth at any time entails its truth at every time, and nothing at the time or afterwards can make it false. Here again we have the criteria of independence and immutability. But, he says, it is incoherent to suppose that it is necessary in the sense that the individual it refers to could not fail to have had the property of existing, or that it is analytic (that is, its negation is incoherent). Hick says that 'it is meaningless to say of the self-existent being that he might not have existed' (*Arguments for the Existence of God,* p. 87), which looks like a stronger sense of necessity; but he means to distinguish this from the view that 'God exists' is a logically necessary truth, on the ground that 'all existential propositions are synthetic'.

Now it does not seem to me meaningless to say that a causally independent and eternal being might not have existed; and that entails that there could have been a universe without such a being, or that there could have been a finite, very powerful, quite wise and moderately good being as the cause of the universe, rather like God but not at all the same being. It is true that if a being is causally independent of all others in principle, then nothing could *cause* it not to exist. (One might note though that this sort of independence appears to be a logical independence, an independence, not as a most general matter of fact, but in principle. Otherwise, what is independent might conceivably not have been. So it seems that supporters of this view are committed to saying that it is a logical truth that God's existence is independent. And that is certainly a truth about a matter of fact.) Nevertheless, if the statement 'God exists' is synthetic, then it can be denied without incoherence. Such a denial is far from meaningless; it has a clear meaning to say that the world exists without God. And that is just the difficulty with this sense of 'factual necessity', as it has been called: namely, that the universe could exist without God, so that he seems to be a gratuitous addition to ontology.

Although I do not wish the question to be viewed as one of how to interpret Aquinas, I think there are considerations in the *Summa Theologiae* which make this sort of interpretation of necessity difficult to sustain. I shall adduce three. First, his argument in the 'Third Way' is obviously meant to be true of any contingent world whatsoever. It cannot be the case, Aquinas argues, that in any possible world everything is contingent; there must be at least one necessary being in each possible world. So he is committed to the view that, if anything contingent exists, then a necessary being exists. He also thinks that this is the same necessary being in each possible world — namely, the one and only God. The fact that, in common with most contemporary philosophers, I do not regard these views as convincingly argued, as they stand, is not relevant here, since I am only trying to see the understanding of 'necessity' which is expressed in the arguments. Now Aquinas also holds to the principle that 'actual existence takes precedence of potential existence' (qu. 3, art. 1). That is, if there are no actual beings, then there can be no possible beings either. Since the existence of any actual beings whatsoever entails God, it follows that, if there is no necessary being, then there are no actual beings, and so no possible beings either. Therefore, if anything at all is possible, the necessary being exists. And obviously, if the necessary being is possible, then it exists. Now this gives a sense of 'necessary' which adds significantly to the properties of independence and eternity. For it entails that there could be no universe without God, that there could be no being very like God instead of God, and that 'God does not exist' is false in every possible world. This is the sense of necessity I am interested in.

The second consideration from Aquinas is his view that the proposition 'God exists' is self-evident in itself (*'in se est per se nota'*; qu. 2, art. 1), though not to us. If a proposition is self-evident, its negation must be incoherent, or plainly false by inspection of the terms. Anyone who could truly comprehend all that God is would see the incoherence of the proposition 'There is no God'. But, since no human mind can grasp all that God is, we can see no incoherence in the proposition; it seems coherent to us, but it is not. One way of saying that the negation of a proposition is incoherent is to say that the proposition is logically necessary. It is not logically necessary in the narrow sense that it follows from the axioms of some formally defined system, like the truths of propositional logic. But there is a broader notion of logical necessity, which has eluded all attempts at precise specification, but which might apply to such truths as the following:

'There is no highest prime number'; 'Minds are not the sorts of things which can have substantial existence'; 'Persons are necessarily embodied': 'Nothing can be red and green all over'; and, most relevantly for the moment, 'There is a being which exists in all possible worlds'.

One might refuse to call such truths (and I do not imply that they are all of the same logical status) 'logically necessary', just on the ground that their negations are not obviously self-contradictory. In that case, one might say that 'There is no God' is logically possible, in that it does not contain a contradiction; yet it is false in all possible worlds. This would still be a very strong sense of 'necessity' — stronger than the natural necessity of events happening in accordance with physical laws, stronger than independence plus eternity. And it would entail that some logically possible states are not *really* possible, not possible in any world. As long as one is clear about this, it does not matter much what one calls it. But I shall speak of the proposition 'God exists' as logically necessary, in the broader sense, thus maintaining the view that a state is only absolutely impossible if it is logically impossible (in the sense of incoherent, of including or entailing a contradiction).

We cannot detect an incoherence either in 'There is no being whose possibility entails its existence' or in 'There is a being whose possibility entails its existence'. Yet, if the former is true, then a necessary being is impossible (if it was possible, it would exist). And if the latter is true, then nothing can exist or even be possible without a necessary being (for if anything is ever possible, it is always possible, and among that array of possibles must be the necessary being, which therefore exists). So either a necessary being is impossible, or it exists. It is only coherent to say, 'There is no God', if God is impossible. We cannot tell for certain whether this is so, and so we can say that here is a proposition which is either necessarily true or necessarily false, though we do not know which. The situation is familiar in mathematics; it should cause no alarm in philosophical theology.

The third consideration from Aquinas is his assertion that it is God's very nature to exist ('*Sua igitur essentia est suum esse*'; qu. 3, art. 4). The argument in that article is that nature and existence cannot be distinguished in God; God is his own existence (*esse*). The relevant Latin terms *essentia, ens* and *esse* are not familiar in modern philosophy. I think it is fair to render them respectively as 'nature — what sort of thing it is', 'thing — that fact that is in existence' and 'the act of existing — that by which anything exists'. On this interpretation, the sort of thing God is cannot be distinguished from the act by which he exists: that is, God would not be the same sort of thing, have the same essence, be the same God, if he did not exercise the act of being, if he did not exist. Of any contingent thing, it is true that it may or may not exist; it may come into being or pass away; it is dependent on other things in many ways. It is just the same sort of thing, whether it exists in reality or not — an existing unicorn is not a different sort of thing from an imaginary unicorn. But God, uniquely, being wholly uncausable, not deriving his existence from any other thing, must be whatever he is underivatively. So he would not have the nature of God, the being *a se,* if he did not exist. The concept of God, that which specifies his nature, logically excludes the possibility of his non-existence, and, if we could understand what God was, we would see how and that this was so.

I take it that Anscombe and Geach would object to this interpretation, since it would entail that 'God exists' is logically necessary, which they deny. But I have held that the inner logic of Aquinas's arguments requires him to find a complete explanation of what is, and that an ultimate contingency, even a timeless and independent one, does not give all that is required. In asking, 'Why is God as he is?', one must refer simply to God himself. And an adequate answer, consonantly with the view that explanation consists in the demonstration of necessity, must be that he could not be other than he is. The possibility of non-existence must be excluded just by the possibility of God. God's possibility, uniquely, entails his actuality, which is the strong sense of necessity I have outlined.

In combating the entailment I allege between 'God's nature (*essentia*) cannot be distinguished from the act by which he is (*esse*)' and 'The possibility of God entails his real existence', Anscombe and Geach, quite rightly, point to a development in Aquinas's views on *ens* and *esse*. But, though, after 1256, he no longer thought of '*esse*' as simply what gives the answer to the question, 'What is there?' ('*An est?*'), I think it is misleading to say, as they do, that he 'explained that what he meant by *esse* had nothing to do with existence that is asserted by affirmative answers to the question "*an est?*"'. One can ask, 'Is there blindness in this eye?', although blindness has no *esse* (it is a privation). One can know that God exists without knowing what God is, at least not very fully; and knowing that God is certainly is a different thing from knowing his nature. Nevertheless, an answer to the question, 'What is there?' has *something to do with esse,* even if one needs further work to distinguish grammatically correct answers from answers truly asserting actual existence, instantiating a real essence. In the two cases just mentioned, one needs to show how blindness is a privation, not truly an individuated essence at all; and one needs to explain how our knowledge of God cannot be direct acquaintance with his nature — though I think Thomas would hold that if, impossibly, we could truly know the sense in which God is, we would thereby know his nature, as 'existence in itself subsistent' ('*suum esse subsistens*'; qu. 7, art. 1). Both things are quite difficult to show, and Thomas devotes much work to doing so.

The third case Anscombe and Geach cite, that Christ has one *esse*, even though 'there being a God is different from there being a man', seems to me to support the interpretation that *esse* is concerned with present-actuality. For although those two things are indeed logically distinct in general, in the case of Christ (for Aquinas) they are indivisibly united in one *'persona'*; in that unique case, two essences are individuated by one act of being, so as to form one indivisible entity, humanity-assumed-into-Godhood. *Esse* is precisely the existence signified by 'there is a . . .'. What is made clear though is that the answer to the question 'What is there?' cannot be any logically possible description; it must take account of the real natures involved, and the manner of their actualization. I conclude that, in speaking of *esse,* Thomas is speaking of what actually exists, as individualized essence; and that, in the case of God, he is saying that the essence is necessarily embodied in an act of existing. It is, perhaps, misleading to speak of this as 'being individualized', since God is the same as his own essence (*'Deus est idem quod sua essentia'*; qu. 3, art. 3), so that his nature cannot logically be instantiated in more than one case; to be God is to be this God. Thus the nature of God can only be instantiated in one case; and it must be instantiated, since it cannot be distinguished from the act by which it is or would be. This is to say that God is a necessary being, in precisely the sense that the proposition 'God exists' is necessarily true. There is no possible world in which God does not exist; so that the negation of the proposition that he exists is incoherent. While the Anscombe–Geach distinction of two senses of 'is' – the 'now actually exists' sense and the 'there is a . . .' sense of existential quantification – is a useful one, it would, I believe, be wrong to suggest that Thomas's use of *'esse'* in the sense of 'now actually existing' does not entail that there is a God. But if it does, then the fact that God's nature entails his *'esse'* does mean that if God is possible, he exists; if God is possible, there is a God.

My argument so far has been that it is a presupposition of the intelligibility of the universe that there is a being which is both self-explanatory and fully explanatory of everything other than itself. I construed the traditional cosmological arguments for God as articulations of this idea. I suggested that a self-explanatory being must be a logically necessary being, in a broad sense of logical necessity, and I defended this notion against various criticisms. It must be uncaused and immutable; it can depend upon nothing other than itself for its existence. Therefore there can be only one being from-itself (*a se*); and, since it must exist in every possible world, we have a logically unique identifying description for God. He is the one and only uncaused, immutable, imperishable, necessarily existent being. The specification of his nature alone entails his existence, and this in turn explains the existence and nature of everything that exists. But this seems to imply that one can deduce the existence of God from the simple possibility of the concept of God. So at this point one must revisit what Kant called the ontological argument for God's existence, at once the simplest, most profound and, to many, most obviously mistaken, argument of all.

2   The Necessarily Existent

Immanuel Kant held that all possible arguments to the existence of God depend upon what he called the ontological argument, and that without it they are quite insufficient to attain their purpose. The argument from design may get one to a supreme architect; the cosmological argument, from contingency to necessity, may get one to a self-existent source of all being. But if one is to establish that this being is the perfectly powerful, wise and good God of theism, something further is needed. How can one ever argue from the finite and limited to the infinite and unlimited? This attempt to jump from the imperfect to the perfect can, it seems, never be justified or corroborated. Kant therefore starts at the other end; not from the fact of imperfect nature, but from the concept of a perfect being. And he tries to establish from the concept alone, the actual existence of such a being. There is no other way, he claims, to establish the existence of an infinitely perfect being; the only possible argument is the purely a priori argument from concepts alone. And in the *First Critique,* he announces that any such argument must necessarily fail. So God is unprovable, as far as speculation is concerned.

The Kantian conclusion is put more brutally by Flew, who says 'It is manifestly preposterous to try to deduce the existence of a thing simply from the definition of a word' (*God and Philosophy,* p. 80). Is it, however, so manifestly absurd? The argument may be stated in a number of different ways, all of them concerned to pin down the idea of what it is to exist necessarily, and to show that this idea entails or is entailed by the idea of perfection. To say that it is a matter of definition is not to say that one is arbitrarily playing around with marks on paper or meaningless words, giving them some quite idiosyncratic definitions. On the contrary, one is attempting to uncover the real meanings of these very puzzling concepts and their logical relations. To discover a meaning requires a reference to perceived reality, but that reference need not be simple or direct. Most of philosophical activity is concerned with analysing the meanings of concepts like 'justice', 'beauty' and 'freedom'. In doing so, one refers to masses of perceived data about the world and human life; but one is not doing experiments. One is attempting to discern patterns, connections and correspondences, organizing one's interpretation of reality by re-orientating concepts in relation to each other. It is not a matter of 'just words'; it is a matter of the fundamental ways in which our concepts enable us to see reality.

The mistake is to think that the theist supposes that by mere argument, he somehow brings God into existence. That would be absurd. The claim is that, by an analysis of certain elements of the conceptual scheme in terms of which we interpret reality, we find that a presupposition of this scheme is the existence of certain types of entity. Thus, by analysis of the notions of 'substance', 'identity' and 'space-time', we may construct an argument to show that the existence of spatial particulars is a necessary condition of our conceptual scheme. We are not proving that objects exist by juggling with words. We are showing that, if we employ these concepts as we do, we presuppose the existence of objects; and the proof proceeds without reference to any particular object.

It is not absurd to think that by analysis of the notions of 'perfection', 'being', 'necessity' and 'existence', one might find that a presupposition of their objective applicability to the world is the existence of an object of a certain type. The proof will proceed without reference to any such particular object, except that, since it turns out that there can logically be only one perfect necessary being, in this case the argument does establish the existence of a particular entity, God. It establishes it, of course, only in the sense that the existence of that object is a necessary condition of the relevant concepts having the sort of application we allege. This will be contested, as will most questions about the application of the centrally puzzling philosophical concepts of substance, freedom, personhood and existence. So the central contested claim is that these concepts do have an application to objective reality. The claim seems to me a reasonable one, but the arguments will never be stronger than the claim which underlies it.

We might see the argument as proceeding in three stages. First, consider the notion of a being which, if it is possible, is actual. We cannot tell if that concept has any application, but it is not self-contradictory nor is it vacuous, since it contradicts the notion of a being which can be possible but not actual. But surely, anything which is actual might not have been actual and yet possible? That, if true, would have to be a necessary truth, and I do not see how it could be proved to be true. It is precisely what is being denied. So I think what we have to say is that we do not know whether it is necessarily true that there could be no being which could be actual but not simply possible and not-actual. In the absence of a proof of that proposition, we are compelled to admit the possibility of the notion of a being which, if it is possible, is actual. But it follows immediately that it is actual. It is a conceptual truth that any possibly necessary being is actual. This is the vital part of the argument Anselm gives in chapter 3 of the *Proslogion*, the so-called 'second version' of his proof.

The second stage of the argument lies in elucidating the idea of a particular possible necessary being. Suppose that it is possible that there is a being which is greater than any other conceivable being. One of the properties such a being will possess will be that of necessary existence. As Descartes puts it, 'Existence can no more be separated from the essence of God than the fact that the three angles of a triangle are together equal to two right angles can be separated from it' (Meditation 5). It is not, however, that 'existence' is a property which a perfect being must possess. Nor is it, as Anselm put it in chapter 2 of *Proslogion*, in the first, less satisfactory, form of his proof, that it is better to exist in reality than to exist as an object of understanding (better to be actual than possible). Both these formulations are open to well-known objections. It is, rather, that the most perfect conceivable being will, besides all its other good properties, possess the property of being self-existent, dependent on itself alone — for it is better to be unchangeable and indestructible by any being, against its will. But what is self-existent must be uncaused, and thus it either exists or it is impossible. If it is possible for it to exist, it must do so; for it cannot be brought into being or simply come into being for no reason. And that is to say that the most perfect conceivable being will be a being which cannot be conceived not to exist. If it is possible, it is actual; it is a necessarily existent being. It follows, by the first part of the argument, that the perfect being exists (and this is what is often called Anselm's 'second' form of the ontological argument).

The third and final stage is to show that there can be only one being which is necessary *a se*, which does not derive its necessity from something else, and this is the perfect being. It is not true, as Kant claims, that 'any limited being whatsoever . . . may also be unconditionally necessary' (*Critique of Pure Reason*, A588). If that were so, the argument to necessity alone would certainly not get one to God. But no limited being can be unconditionally necessary; for, by the very fact of having limits, of being limited by some other being, it depends for its nature on that other being, and so can only be at best conditionally necessary. One might say that an object could retain the same properties, even while its antecedent conditions vary; so that it might be necessary, whatever its antecedents. But then such an object would be outside the causal nexus of the universe. Its nature would have to follow simply from itself. It would, in short, be self-existent.

By the first part of the argument, all possible necessary beings actually exist (it is quite clear that if they do not exist in this world, they cannot exist in every possible world, and so are contingent, by definition). By the second part of the argument, the most perfect conceivable being is a necessary being; so it exists. By the third part, any underivatively necessary being must be a self-existent being. As we saw in chapter 1, there can only be one self-existent being. So there can only be one being whose necessity does not derive from another, which is unlimited by anything other than itself. Since all other necessary beings are only derivatively so, and such derivation, being existential, is irreflexive, they must derive their being from the self-existent, which is the only being which exists by unconditional necessity. Clearly, the perfect being is identical with the uniquely self-existent being, for it is better to be underived in existence than to depend upon another. Therefore the perfect being is the only underivatively necessary being, and it actually exists.

It is therefore no reply to the ontological argument to say that perfect fairies or islands may exist necessarily, and thus must be actual (as Gaunilo did). Such things can only exist by necessity if they are unlimited in their existence by anything outside themselves; whereas they are obviously not. They must be such that their existence follows from their concept alone, without reference to anything else. Since they exist without reference to anything but themselves, they must be identical with the uniquely self-existent first cause of all being. So there can, after all, be only one unconditionally necessary being, the unlimited first cause of all.

What is supposed to be distinctive about the ontological argument is that it starts simply from an idea, the idea of a greatest conceivable being, and concludes that this idea must be instantiated, since any such being, and only such a being, exists by unconditional necessity. Kant argues that all other arguments for God must presuppose and rely upon this one, since, without it, one cannot show that the architect or first cause of the world is perfect. But it would be a serious misrepresentation to suppose that one is just assuming an arbitrary definition — say, 'the idea of a being which cannot fail to exist' — and deducing analytically that such a being exists, as though it was just a piece of verbal juggling. What is in question is the understanding of reality which certain concepts enable one to have, and the adequacy of those concepts for integrating and organizing one's experience coherently. One needs to analyse the notion of a perfect being, to see if it is coherent, and what it implies. One needs to examine the concept of 'necessity', to see whether and how it can apply to realities. And one needs to see how various notions of explanation, value and interpretation of experience flow from the analysis one proposes.

The sorts of reflection involved in understanding the ontological argument are the same as those involved in assessing the other arguments for God; they require the same, indirect, reference to the nature of reality; the same reliance on a priori structures of interpretation; the same checking for adequacy of the resultant conceptual scheme. Indeed, one may well reverse Kant's verdict, and say that the ontological argument, being the most abstract and general of all, presupposes and relies upon all the other forms of argument for God which lie hidden in it.

The cosmological arguments do not infer a supremely self-determining being from observation of the world in general. The idea of total intelligibility is brought to experience as a regulative principle for its methodical investigation, and grounded in the postulate of the necessary self-existent. The idea has, as Kant puts it, objective but indeterminate validity; it may, for all we know, grossly exaggerate the rational unity of the world. There are certainly features of the world which suggest the existence of God. There are traces of purpose, universality, unity, continuity and necessity in nature, as well as moral obligations and the feelings of dependence, dialogue and personal presence which characterize theistic experience. But to get to belief in God one has to explore the presuppositions of a coherently worked-out conceptual scheme which can include all these factors within one intelligible framework. It is not a matter of inductive inference, but of a constant search for the coherent formulation of underlying rational structures. What theistic arguments do is suggest a hypothetical structure in the light of which the world would be a rational and meaningful totality. This structure may be suggested by many particular experiences, focusing on many aspects of perceived reality, but it remains an a priori and rational construction.

So one arrives, as a result of reflection on various aspects of the world, at a putatively coherent idea of a God, as possessing the basic perfections of a uniquely self-determining being. It remains, however, a postulate, an a priori model suggested, but not entailed by, our moral and intellectual commitments and interpretations. Are these arguments, then, different in kind from the ontological? The sense in which they begin from experience is only the sense in which the phenomena of purpose and causality serve as starting-points for a meditative reflection, generating the regulative postulate of a self-existent first cause. The ontological argument requires a similar reference to experiences of value in order to generate the idea of the greatest (most valuable) conceivable being. It requires a general assessment of the plausibility of supposing that the universe is a product of a perfect being, just as the other arguments require some confirmation of purpose and intelligible causality in the universe. Though this element is not often stressed in considering the argument, it is clear that, if the universe was believed to be intrinsically evil, any argument that a perfect being must exist would be weakened or destroyed. Either the coherence of the concept or the coherence and objective applicability of the notion of 'necessary existence' would have to be denied.

The structure of the argument in the so-called cosmological and ontological proofs is thus essentially the same. Both are arguments which are primarily philosophical, not experimental: that is to say, they are concerned with analysis of certain concepts, especially those of 'necessity', 'causality', 'explanation' and 'value'. This is not just a matter of defining terms at will, but of trying to achieve a coherent, consistent, elegant and illuminating conceptual interpretation of reality. Just as the verification principle was an attempt to express a reasonable and consistent attitude to reality which would be adequate to all sorts of possible experience, so the axiom of intelligibility upon which rational theism relies is an attempt to do the same thing. The difference lies in the basic model of the world: in one case it is seen as a collection of contingently related atomic data; in the other as a rational whole with a necessary structure. That difference cannot be decided inductively, or by any neutral decision-procedure. So a 'proof' of the existence of God, the self-explanatory being, is not a chain of reasoning which anyone who understands logic must accept. It is more like a philosophical proof of the existence of sense-data, or of substantival minds. The conclusion cannot be checked by experiment; it follows from the proposal and articulation of a certain way of understanding reality, expressed in a specific conceptual system.

Such metaphysical conjectures do not derive inductively from experience, but they are related to experience in two ways. First, they are suggested by reflection on certain aspects of experience — on causality, for the cosmological proofs, and on value, for the ontological argument. This suggests, in the one case, the postulate of the completely satisfactory causal explanation, and, in the other, the postulate of the most valuable or perfect conceivable being. There is no inference in either case, but contemplated experience suggests the models of the self-explanatory and of the perfect, respectively. Then there is a second sort of reference to experience when one checks one's postulate against what actually occurs, to see if it is adequate. One tries to see if the universe, as investigated by the sciences, does seem amenable to reason, if it is intelligible. And one tries to see if it is the sort of universe a perfect being might produce, especially in view of the existence of evil and ugliness. In the end such conjectures differ from those of scientific conjectures in that they are not strictly falsifiable by a decisive experiment. Yet they are falsifiable in a looser way, by lack of coherence, adequacy or simplicity. The existence of unintelligible phenomena, incapable of being assimilated under general laws, throws doubt on the axiom of intelligibility, and thus greatly weakens an argument to God as self-explanatory being. The existence of great suffering, incapable of justification, throws doubt on the axiom of value, and thus greatly weakens an argument to God as perfect being. In each case, there is nothing wrong with the arguments, but one would be inclined to reject the underlying supposition that reason is capable of giving truth about the structure of reality, that speculative metaphysics is possible.

I think this is what lies behind the first reaction of most contemporary thinkers to the ontological argument: namely, that, however convincing it might appear, it could not work and must be verbal trickery. One cannot prove that reality is intelligible, though, if it is, God exists. One cannot prove that the notion of a perfect being, in the sense of a being which cannot fail to exist, is coherent; though, if it is, the perfect being, God, exists. Nevertheless, the ontological argument depends upon the cosmological argument in this way: the latter shows that, given an assumption of intelligibility, there is a self-explanatory being, so the notion of such a being must be a coherent one. It is not that the cosmological proof starts with a ready-made concept of God, which it then shows to be instantiated.. Rather, it develops a coherent concept of God, in the course of arguing to the presupposition of intelligibility. Now this is a major part of the idea of a perfect being, so it strongly supports the claim that the idea of a perfect being is coherent. I shall argue later that in a similar way the design argument argues to the existence of an intrinsically valuable being from a supposition of purposive causality. In doing so, it articulates the notion of such a being and shows it to be coherent. This provides the second major element in the idea of a perfect being, a being which is self-existent and of maximal intrinsic value. Thus, taken together, these arguments strongly support the view that the idea of a perfect being is coherent. At this stage, the ontological proof argues from coherence to actual existence. And now, of course, the existence of such a being justifies the first assumptions of intelligibility, value and purpose.

The circle is complete. On the assumption of intelligibility, the idea of God is coherent; by the ontological proof, if God is coherent then he exists; and if God exists, the assumption of intelligibility is justified. Kant was wrong in thinking that the ontological proof did not need the others, and that they could not give support to the idea of God without it. But he was right in thinking that the proof has a peculiar importance; it makes it quite clear that the question about the existence of God is not about a contingent matter of fact, which may or may not exist. The idea of God is the idea of a being which is either existent or impossible; the decision as to which it is must be made of the basis of a great many cumulative arguments about value, intelligibility, purpose and freedom in the universe. The circle of theistic argument is not vicious, but one can refuse to enter it. Kant himself, in a rather peculiar sense, did so.

After his discovery of the antinomies of pure reason, which seemed to lead reason into irresolvable contradictions, Kant denied that reason alone could discover the nature of reality. The objective existence of a being corresponding to our concepts can never be established in the absence of possible experience. So no argument to a being beyond experience, much less an argument which does not even seem to start from experience, can possibly succeed. So much of

Kant's doctrine is well known. He has often been interpreted as the 'all-destroyer', demolishing all possible arguments for the existence of God. But Kant never gave up his basic rationalism, and with the aid of his doctrine of transcendental idealism he was able to preserve it in a revised form. The demands of reason remain absolute, but they become regulative postulates, necessary ideas whose objective validity we are unable to establish, but whose necessity for thought is unquestionable. So God, as the 'Ideal of Reason', is an absolutely necessary hypothesis, something which we must think if we are to maintain the rational intelligibility of the world. In the *Lectures on Philosophical Theology*, given for many years after the *Critique of Pure Reason* and thus representing a post-Critical stage of his thought, he repeats a proof of God which he had given in one of his earliest works, the *Beweisgrund,* and says of it, 'This proof only establishes the subjective necessity of such a being. That is, our speculative reason sees that it is necessary to presuppose this being if it wants to have insight into why something is possible. But the objective necessity of such a thing can by no means be demonstrated' (*Lectures on Philosophical Theology,* p. 68). While he was concerned to deny the possibility of apodictic proof of God, he was equally concerned to defend the necessity of the regulative postulate of God.

The proof which he gives is an interesting analysis of the notion of a 'necessary being'. It may be construed as follows: To say that A exists necessarily is to say that, in every possible world, A exists. That is, if anything is possible, A is actual. It follows deductively from this that, if A is not actual, nothing is possible. The non-existence of A would entail the absence of any possibilities. But where nothing is possible, nothing is thinkable, since one can only think what is possible. Thus the non-existence of God is strictly unthinkable and inconceivable. We may utter the statement 'A does not exist', and it does not appear to be self-contradictory. But in fact A is the being without which nothing would be possible. In saying 'A does not exist', one is, however, trying to conceive of a possible state of affairs, the state in which there is no A. That state is precisely a state in which nothing is possible, so one is committed to saying that it is possible that nothing is possible. Since such a statement combines the incompatible statements that 'one thing is possible' and that 'nothing is possible', it is self-contradictory. So the non-existence of a necessary being is self-contradictory. It follows, of course, that the being *a se* exists.

That God is a being without which there would be no possibilities not only follows from the definition of a necessary being. It is also directly derivable from the notion of a totally explanatory being, when considered in relation to possibility in general. God, the self-explanatory being, must also explain the existence of everything other than himself. Both their existence and their nature must derive from him. If possibilities exist, therefore, their existence and nature must derive from God and cannot be independent. Otherwise something could be possible — that is, could become actual — for which God could not be wholly responsible; so he could not constitute its final explanation. Moreover, there cannot exist something that is merely possible — a possible thing is no sort of existent thing. So, if there are real possibilities, they must have their being within some actual thing; as Aquinas puts it, 'Actual existence takes precedence of potential existence' (*Summa Theologiae*, qu. 3, art. 1). Many possibilities necessarily exist; therefore they must exist in some actual being, and that actual being must be God or wholly dependent upon God, who is accordingly correctly conceived as '*ens realissimum*', the origin and conceiver of all possibilities. If one asks what a necessary being could be, the answer is that it is that being which is the ground of all possibilities. The specification of his nature defines the whole realm of possibility and constitutes him as the actual ground of that realm.

Kant's view is that we must assume such a being, an *ens*

realissimum; it 'remains an ideal free from faults, anchoring and crowning the whole of human knowledge: (*Lectures,* p. 69). But we cannot assert that it exists in objective reality; the inescapably hidden nature of the *ding-an-sich* prevents us from making any such assertion; and no example could be found within experience. Kant's refusal to enter the theistic circle is peculiar, because he retains the structure of rationalist thought, while denying that reality in itself corresponds to that structure. But if one assumes that reality is rational, and that the mind is capable of tracing the elements of this rationality in its own structures of thought, even a priori arguments may entail existential conclusions. If one does not accept Kant's general doctrine of transcendental idealism, that space and time and all the basic structures of thought about the natural world are products of the mind, the chief reason for denying ideas of reason any objective validity disappears. It is, after all, extremely odd to suggest that it may be necessary for us to think of the world as *x,* while at the same time denying that it need be *x.* If our thought is necessary, we cannot at the same time say that it is not really necessary.

The case is similar with Kant's doctrine that the concept of causality (and indeed of necessity, too) is vacuous when used outside sense-experience, so that one cannot argue to a transcendent or first cause of the world, which is not part of the endless series of caused causes in the world. This depends on an assertion that one can only argue from effect to cause in cases where the inference can be independently checked by direct inspection of the cause. So any inference to an unobservable cause is invalid. What is called for is a rejection of the premiss. It is not analytic to the notion of 'cause' that causes must be observable; and if an inference to an unobservable cause is required as a condition of the possibility of the total intelligibility of the world, it is legitimate. Indeed, as has been widely noticed, Kant himself is forced to use the categories of existence, causality, substance and possibility

transcendentally, when he states that there is, or even that
there may be or that we must act as if there were, a nou-
menal world, underlying the phenomenal world of our knowledge.

But one may go further than Kant, and reject rationalism
in principle, denying that any moves made by reason can give
either knowledge or even necessary regulative belief. It is at
this point that the gap becomes unbridgeable, for one cannot
prove that the world is rational or that our reason accurately
describes its structure. One can only argue that science and
common sense may seem to suppose its rationality; and
religious belief, as belief in an objective ethical purpose, in
the ultimate co-incidence of reason, value and purpose, finds
its ultimate object in the God so specified. That is the context in which these speculative proofs carry conviction: as
explorations of the idea of the unique self-explanatory being
which is the completely self-determining and wholly explanatory cause of the world.

It may seem that this argument is of remote interest to
religious life, that the God of the philosophers is, as Pascal
observed, very different from the God of Abraham, Isaac and
Jacob. It is true that the argument depends upon no great
mystical or visionary experience, yet it is of vital importance
to the believer. For no devout worshipper of God could
admit that God could derive his being from another; thus he
must be self-existent. And none could admit that God might
be less perfect than some other being; thus he must be maximally valuable. It is, as Anselm saw, as a result of prayerful
meditation that one sees that the God who is the object of
worship must be 'that than which no greater can be conceived', the self-existent and perfect cause of all. The thought
that God might be just a superior limited being, that he
might just happen to be wise and good, that he might be a
contingently existing creator, instead of the standard and unsurpassable ground of all beings; that thought is deeply repugnant to the religious consciousness. So the requirements of

rational intelligibility are also the requirements of the quest for the ultimate source and goal of being, the only satisfying resting place for the person who worships. This consideration would not have appealed much to Kant, from whose works any conception of worship seems conspicuously absent. But it is of great interest to the believer that the notions of rational intelligibility and of the object of worship are closely intertwined, so that theism is indeed the crown of reason, and not at all a blind and unjustifiable leap of faith.

If Kant's 'Copernican revolution' must itself be overturned, so that we may again grant reason the ability to discern the nature of reality truly, his most basic objection to the ontological proof disappears — the objection which so many moderns repeat, without having any disposition to accept the doctrine of transcendental idealism upon which it is based. The objection was that human thinking cannot meaningfully transcend sense-experience; to which the reply is that such a restriction has never been adequately justified, while both physicists and theists appear to do just that while understanding one another well enough. Kant's own justification of the restriction — the doctrine of transcendental idealism — rarely finds favour. In default of a stronger one, I suggest we ignore the restriction.

His more particular objections to the ontological argument, in the *First Critique,* fare no better — as he appears to have seen, in ignoring them when he gave his lectures on religion in later years. Yet they have been widely influential, and it is instructive to consider them. His main attack is on the idea of 'necessary existence'.

Is the notion of a necessary being, a being which could not fail to exist, and which contains the reason for its existence in itself, a coherent one? If it is not, the whole argument I have constructed falls to the ground, for it depends upon the possibility of a self-explanatory being, which must be, as has been seen, a necessary being. The coherence of the idea of a necessary being has seemed obvious to a great many philosophers: Aristotle, Anselm, Aquinas, Leibniz, Descartes, Spinoza and Hegel made it an important keystone in their systems of metaphysics. Yet it has come under attack in more recent times, most notably by Hume and Kant, and philosophers in the analytic tradition. J. N. Findlay said bluntly that, because theism is committed to asserting the necessary existence of God, 'the Divine existence is either senseless or impossible' (*New Essays in Philosophical Theology*, p. 54), though he subsequently changed his mind, and came to accept the coherence of the idea of necessary existence. Necessarily true propositions, he claims, are, at least on 'modern' views, only arbitrary conventions, merely linguistic, and so irrelevant to the facts. In Kant's phrase, 'Necessity of judgements is not the same as an absolute necessity of things' (*Critique of Pure Reason* A594). All real necessity is conditional, stating that if x, then necessarily y; if a triangle has three sides on a plane surface, then its angles add up to 180 degrees. But that necessary connection depends upon a mathematical convention, which can easily be changed — and is, in Riemannian and other geometries. So, one can say, 'If God exists, then he is necessarily omnipotent', as long as one is clear that one is *defining* God in that way. But one cannot say that the proposition 'God exists' is necessarily true, unless one means that one is determined to assert it, whatever the facts may be. No existential assertion can be necessary, because all necessary propositions are true by convention only, and no existential assertion is true simply by convention — so runs the argument.

The argument depends upon two related axioms: that there are no necessary connections in objective reality, and that there are no non-conventional necessary truths. But suppose one simply says 'There are necessary connections in the world, and any proposition which states them is necessarily true'. Has one just run up against a blank wall? Not quite; because the objector will go on to ask what exactly is meant by 'necessary'. If one says that some laws of nature are necessary, does one mean that they could not be otherwise, that their contradiction is incoherent? Or does one just mean that, given the general nature of the universe, they will not change, that they are, perhaps, physically but not logically necessary? Many philosophers would hold that particular causal relations are physically necessary; the apple must fall to the ground, in quite determinate ways, as long as the inverse square law holds. Yet that law is not itself necessary; there could have been an inverse cube law instead. Well, if the laws of nature are not absolutely necessary, is anything? The usual candidates offered are truths about God, morality and logic, and perhaps some very general truths about the world — that there must be relatively necessary causal connections, for example, without specifying what they must be exactly. It is necessary, one might say, that in any possible world there must be some rational structure, and thus some generally applicable laws. There must be a preponderance of good over evil, and there must be a tendency towards some valuable purpose. If so, the propositions stating these facts must be necessarily true.

But now the objector has something hard to grip on. 'Surely', he will say, 'It cannot be necessarily true that there must be a valuable purpose in any possible universe'. For to say that is to deny the very possibility of atheism or of a purposeless world, and such a thing is surely possible, even if not actual. Yet of course this is precisely what the theist wishes to deny; in asserting that God is necessary, the theist does precisely want to say that a purposeless world is impossible. 'But', pursues the objector, 'The only real ground you can have for saying that something is impossible is if it is self-contradictory or vacuous. And a world without purpose, or the non-existence of God, is not self-contradictory or vacuous. In fact, it is widely believed and asserted by millions of people'. David Hume put this argument in a brief dismissive comment in the *Dialogues* (pt. 9), in support of the view that, if 'God exists' is necessarily true, then 'God does not exist' must be necessarily false, i.e. self-contradictory. He says, 'Whatever we conceive as existent, we can also conceive as non-existent. There is no being, therefore, whose non-existence implies a contradiction.' We can conceive of God not existing quite coherently; what we can conceive, can be; therefore God may not exist; therefore he cannot exist necessarily.

This argument is not as shattering as has been sometimes supposed. There are notorious difficulties in Hume's concept of 'conceiving'. Does he mean 'imagine', as if one was to picture to oneself an actual instantiation of the concept? Or does he mean simply 'form a concept of'? In either case, it is quite possible to frame concepts of things, or imagine things, even though we are unable to tell whether they are possible or not. One can say, 'It is possible to travel backwards in time', and can frame the concepts which go to make up that assertion; one can even imagine time-travel. Similarly, one can imagine travelling faster than the speed of light. But does it follow that it is possible, even logically, to do such things? If one could clearly understand all that was involved in such assertions, it might turn out that they involve incoherencies, about the reversability of time, for example. It is certainly possible that, though we can clearly think of time-travel, there is, unknown to us, a logical contradiction involved in the idea of going back in time. Some philosophers have argued that logical contradictions are involved in the idea of disembodied minds, or of life after death; yet others believe such things are clearly possible. At the very least, it is not true that our claim to conceive something shows that it does not contain a logical contradiction. This is presumably because it is very difficult indeed, and perhaps in some cases impossible, to know when even seemingly quite clear conceptions are coherent.

The best examples of all come from mathematics, where they abound. To take just one well-known case: Goldbach's Conjecture, that every even number greater than 2 is the sum of two primes, was formulated in 1742. Being a proposition in pure mathematics, it is agreed that, if it is true, it is necessarily true, so its denial is self-contradictory. Yet it has never been proved; so it may conceivably be false, even though it is true over every case which has ever been tried, to millions of numbers. Here we have a case in which a proposition 'There is some number which is even and greater than 2, which is not the sum of two primes' is either self-contradictory or true; we cannot demonstrate either, but we may believe, and frame the concept of, either case. Again, we may conceive something which may well be (probably is, in this case) self-contradictory. A similar case which used to exist was the contention that some square could be found, equal in area to any given circle. This has now been proved to be impossible, that is, self-contradictory. But mathematicians tried for years to 'square the circle', and a great many believed it could be done.

In an analogous way, the theist may say that Hume may very well be able to conceive of God not existing and to believe there is no God; but that in no way shows that what he conceives is not self-contradictory. He does not, of course, see it to be contradictory, but seeing contradictions is no easy matter, as mathematicians and philosophers must ruefully admit. To follow the lead of mathematics just a little further, one may be able to prove the unprovability of certain theorems, that is, to show conclusively that they cannot be established as necessarily true, even though they are or may be so. So God may necessarily exist, even though it is in principle impossible to demonstrate that conclusively. There may be theological reasons why this should be so, to do with the mystery and ineffability of the Divine being or the limitations of the human intellect. Perhaps the notion of God will be made precise and then be shown to be contradictory, as was eventually shown in the case of squaring circles. That is a risk the theist takes. But it has not yet been done. After all, if one can meaningfully say, 'contingent existence', there is a prima facie case for forming a meaningful proposition simply by the addition of the negative operator, which does not in general suffice to make sensible statements into gibberish. So one has 'non-contingent existence' as a logically possible statement, and one would need very strong arguments to show why this simple grammatical change does not produce simple good sense. Hume's arguments are not very strong; they are virtually non-existent.

Of course one can *say,* 'God does not exist', just as we can say, 'God could not fail to exist'. But unless we know precisely what 'God' means, we cannot say which proposition embodies a self-contradiction; certainly one of them must, if the other is true. Richard Swinburne has recently tried an elaboration of Hume's argument, pointing out that the contradictory of any statement entailed by a necessary statement must be inconsistent. But 'God exists' entails 'There exists a being which knows more than I do'; and 'There does not exist any being which knows more than I do', though pretty clearly false, does not seem to be inconsistent. So the notion of a necessary existent is, after all, incoherent.

At first, this looks convincing; for it seems strange to say that 'No being exists which knows more than I do' is self-contradictory. Taken on its own, of course, it does not contradict itself. It is necessarily false, not because the phrase contains a self-contradiction, but because it contradicts another assertion which is necessarily true, namely, 'There is an omniscient being'. To see that the phrase is necessarily false, one must see that it contradicts 'There is an omniscient being', and that the latter phrase is entailed by one that is necessarily true; it is not enough simply to look hard at the statement itself. However, there is no reason at all why necessarily false statements should be obviously so, as we have seen. So it is no argument against 'There is no one wiser than I' being necessarily false, that it obviously seems to be coherent, taken in isolation from all statements which entail or are entailed by it (like 'There is no perfectly wise being').

To say that 'God exists' is logically necessary is not to trivialize the concept of God by making his existence a matter of verbal definition. 'God exists' is not made true by any arbitrary set of axioms. It is made true by the existence of God, and what makes it non-contingent is that there is no possible world in which God does not exist. I conclude that the notion of a logically necessary being is a coherent one, and if this could be demonstrated, it would follow that any such being would exist. Existence will be a necessary property of such a being.

This statement will immediately raise the hackles of all who remember Kant's obscure dictum that 'being is obviously not a real predicate' (*Critique of Pure Reason* A598). Existence, it has been said, is not a property at all, so it cannot logically be possessed by anything. In saying that *x* exists, we are not attaching a predicate to a subject. We are doing something quite different: saying that something in reality corresponds to a concept, that there is a subject which can possess various properties. What, after all, would 'existence' be a property of? It could not be of an existent subject, which would beg the question. In G. E. Moore's famous example ('Is Existence a Predicate?', *Proceedings of the Aristotelian Society,* supp. vol. 1963), we can say, 'All tame tigers growl' and 'Some tame tigers do not growl'. But it seems senseless to say, 'All tame tigers exist' and 'Some tame tigers do not exist'. In order to ascribe any properties at all, one must presuppose an existent subject, to which they can be ascribed; and if existence is presupposed to the ascription of any properties at all, it cannot itself be a property.

When Kant says that 'being' is not a real predicate, he means that it is not a determining predicate, one that is added to the concept of the subject and enlarges it. It may indeed seem that 'being' is not a property like 'yellowness' or 'size', which adds to the description of an object. I do not add to the description of £100 by saying that it exists. Yet, of course, I do say something about my £100, and something rather complicated, when I say that it exists. Kant's point is perhaps that to define a concept is to describe a possible thing. If that is so, one cannot have, as part of the description of a merely possible thing, that it is actual. When I say, 'X exists', I am not adding to the concept; I am saying that some object corresponds to the concept; and that statement is always a synthetic one, not given by analysis of the concept itself.

This is an odd doctrine, since Kant defines a synthetic judgement as one that 'adds to the concept of the subject a predicate which has not been in any way thought in it' (*Critique of Pure Reason*, A7). He seems to be caught in an overt contradiction. When he tries to construe what it means to say that 'X exists', he offers the thought that the object of my thought belongs to the context of experience, as a possible object of perception. But is not 'being a possible object of perception' a property? Naturally, the fact that I think of £100 as being perceivable, spendable and so on does not show that it is; what I think may not exist (that is, may not really be perceivable). But, if my £100 is real, being perceivable will be a property of it. 'Being perceivable' is not, of course, a property of any concept; concepts are not perceivable. But it is certainly a property of the object I am thinking of. In a similar way, I do not add to my description of Socrates when I say that he is alive. But 'being alive' is a property he once had, and now no longer has. It is a very important fact about him, not least to him. I am saying something about him when I say that he exists; and why should I not say that I am ascribing (truly or falsely) the property of 'being alive', or of 'existing', to him?

It seems that 'existence' need not be a property of objects, because I can think about things that do not exist. I do not even have to think of them as existing — they may be purely imaginary, extinct or illusory. So when I do think of them as existing, my thought-content carries an additional quality or element. Kant's rather lame argument against this is that if 'existence' added something to the original concept of a thing, then it would not be that original concept, the object of which was said to exist; it would be a new, enlarged, concept. But, as Jerome Shaffer has pointed out ('Existence, Predication and the Ontological Argument', *Mind,* July 1962), this argument would show that nothing could be a real predicate. For every property, in adding to the concept of something, would change that concept, and so, by this odd argument, would not ascribe the new property to 'the exact object of my concept'.

On Kant's own terms, then, 'existence' does seem to be a real predicate. What remains is the sheer feeling that one cannot, by analysis of a concept, get to actual existence. That is, in general, true. But if it is possible for there to be something which could not fail to exist, the negation of which is incoherent, then in that case, and only in that case, thinking that something is so does prove that it is so; for its denial is self-contradictory. We cannot be certain that there is a possible being, the non-existence of which is self-contradictory. For, as Kant says, 'I cannot form the least concept of a thing which, should it be rejected with all its predicates, leaves behind a contradiction' (*Critique of Pure Reason,* A596). That is an exaggeration; for I can conceive of a perfect, self-existent ground of all possibles, without which nothing could be. Clearly, there could be a being with such properties. But if there could be, then something possible exists, and consequently the self-existent being exists in every possible world; its non-existence would leave nothing possible. Nevertheless, I cannot be certain that my conception is really coherent, and that is the weakness of the ontological proof.

There is thus very little of force in Kant's particular objections to the argument; his best-known arguments are the weakest of all. 'Existence' is obviously a property with distinctive features. As Moore's tame tigers bring out, it is not a property which belongs to already existing or subsisting things. We get referential tautology or referential contradiction when we say such things as, 'All the tigers there are exist' or 'There are some tigers which do not exist'. Yet it is not at all odd to say that some tigers exist and some (imaginary, fictional, dead or illusory ones) do not. In this respect, 'existence' is analogous to properties like 'being extended', which cannot belong to objects existing independently without them, but which do not belong to all possible objects. 'Existing' constitutes something as an actual, real object, just as 'being extended' constitutes a thing as a material object.

Perhaps the most influential modern treatment of 'existence' is Russell's formalization of first-order quantification theory. He holds that 'existence' is a property, but a property of propositional functions (like 'x is a man'), not of objects. So to say, 'There is a God' will be formalized as ' "x is a God" is sometimes true'. 'There is an everlasting God' will be 'For every time t, 'x is a God' is sometimes true, that is, is true at least once'. On this theory, 'being sometimes true' is an undefined predicate of a propositional function. One may easily transpose the doctrine I have defended in such terms. Then, 'There is an everlasting and necessary God, will be something like, 'For all possible worlds, and for every time in those worlds, 'x is a God' is true at least once'. This is virtually equivalent to, ' "x is a God" is always true', which is Russell's definition of a necessary propositional function, which turns into a proposition when some value is substituted for 'x'. And to say that it is always true that there is an individual which is God entails that the idea of a being which exists in every possible world is coherent. That is to embrace at least the first stage of the much-derided ontological argument. And it gives the form in which Alvin Plantinga has given his own version of the argument (*The Nature of Necessity*, p. 216), namely, that, if it is logically possible (sometimes true) that 'x is a maximally excellent being' is always true (true in every possible world), then it is always true, and there is such a being. It is problematic how far the apparatus of first-order quantification theory adequately expresses the ordinary senses of 'existence'. It is, after all, an artificial and formalized language, and, as Anscombe and Geach have stressed, it does not really cover the sense of 'exist' as 'being presently actual'. But any such reservations can only strengthen the point that the idea of necessary existence cannot be ruled out on the ground of some supposed logical incoherence it contains. No such incoherence has been established.

The attraction of the ontological argument is that it expresses the extreme limit of the human attempt to probe the rational structure of reality. It is the analysis of the idea of a most perfect conceivable being, which is self-existent, necessary cause of all, possessing all perfections in its unsurpassable richness of being. Its failure lies in the inability of the human mind to frame a coherent and adequate conceptual interpretation of reality in its full range and depth. Its incompleteness lies in the abstractness of its form, which requires fuller specification by a whole range of cumulative arguments, constructing a particular interpretation of the world as intelligible, purposive and valuable. Its success lies in its demonstration that God is either existent or impossible; that, if a perfect being is possible, then it necessarily exists. The idea of necessary existence has been defended against various attacks. But what about the coherence of the idea of a perfect being? It is not yet clear what such a being would be, whether it is coherently conceivable. I will consider next the traditional notion of the Divine perfection, and suggest that, when appropriately modified, it is indeed a coherent idea.

3   Perfection

It has been widely held among philosophical theologians that, if there is a cause from which the world derives, then that cause must be more perfect than any of its effects. The argument is presented in Aquinas's 'Fourth Way', based on the gradations observed in things. In the world, some things are better than others; but comparative terms all approximate to a superlative; 'something therefore is the truest and best and most noble of things' (*Summa Theologiae*, qu. 2, art. 3). Since the cause must be greater than its effects, this 'best of beings' must be the cause of all lesser perfections; and this is God.

The assertion that, where there are degrees of goodness, there must actually exist some absolute goodness, does not seem very plausible. One may have faster or less fast race-horses, without having any absolutely fast horse. As this example suggests, the idea of absolute goodness is not itself very clear, and may be vacuous. And it is by no means clear that the absolute goodness, whatever that is, must be the cause of any lesser degrees of goodness found in things. This is the least convincing of Aquinas's proofs, as it stands. It relies fundamentally on the principle that the greater cannot come from the less; that causes must be like their effects and at least as great in degree. If that is so, then the first cause of everything (established by the First and Second Ways) must be like everything, in some way, and be at least as great as any of its possible effects. Moreover, there can be no un-realized possibilities in God. For, *ex hypothesi*, such a possi-bility could not be actualized except by something which was already actual in that respect, and, since God is the first cause, that thing would have to be God. Therefore God is actually all that he could ever be; there is nothing he could be that he is not. So God actually is the greatest possible being in every respect: 'The perfections of everything exist in God ... because effects obviously pre-exist potentially in their causes' (*Summa Theologiae,* qu. 4, art. 2). Yet it is clearly unacceptable to say that all things pre-exist in God in just the same way, as a sort of duplicate universe; this would generate an infinite regress of worlds, which is absurd. They must therefore exist in a higher manner — *'eminentiorem modum'* — not as diverse and often opposed, but in an immaterial unity.

Before examining the conclusion, one must ask if there is any reason to accept the basic principle that causes must be like their effects, and at least as great. One might say that if the cause is truly and fully to explain its effects, then the effects must not contain radically new kinds or degrees of any property, for the newness, springing from nothing, would be unexplained. A world springing from nothing would be totally inexplicable. So it may be suggested that a property quite unlike anything previously existing either in degree or in kind would similarly be from nothing, and so inexplicable.

Now it is true that if there can be a wholly explanatory being, it must, by examination of its own self-subsistent nature alone, explain the existence of everything that does or could come into being. If there was anything for which no such explanation could be given, the whole system would collapse; for there might be any number of such things, if their existence cannot be controlled by the necessary being. So it seems natural to conclude that no radically new qualities could come into being. Whatever comes to be must be wholly explicable from the first cause, and so must be derivable from its concept. If one cannot derive anything from the concept of x unless that thing is already implicit or included in the concept of x, then it does follow that the first cause must contain in itself, at least implicitly or in some way, every property that ever comes to be.

By the same argument, that one cannot derive from x what is not already included in it, the first cause must possess the logically maximal degree of every possible property; for nothing can come to be (therefore nothing is possible) unless the first cause brings it into being. God is thus omnipotent, in possessing a degree of power greater than any other logically possible power, a power which nothing outside himself can limit (for there can be no such thing), and which is limited internally only by the bounds of logical possibility (whatever God cannot do is not even logically possible, since he is the ground of all possibilities). God is omniscient, for he must actually possess more knowledge than any other being which could possibly be brought to be. And God is perfectly wise and good and happy, more wise, good and happy than any other possible being, and incapable of being surpassed in these properties even by himself, or another god in another possible world, for he is immutable, so cannot surpass himself. And he is necessary, so must exist as he does in all possible worlds, as the 'best of all'.

On this Anselmian and Thomist argument, the uncaused cause of all created things must be a logically perfect being; it cannot be limited or imperfect in any way. Its only limits are the limits of logical possibility which it contains. It possesses the maximal degree of every possible property. Yet this conclusion, desirable though it is for the theist, carries with it a hidden drawback.

The demands of rational intelligibility lead to the notion of one necessary, self-subsistent being, fully explaining everything that necessarily derives from it, because containing eminently in itself the maximal form of every possible property. This demand is corroborated by the demand of worship for an object which is unsurpassably perfect and changelessly existent, the Eternal which gives value, purpose and meaning to this world of apparent change and decay. Unfortunately, just at this point, when the final object of reason and religion offers to reveal itself in all its glory to the seeking mind, it collapses into incoherence. The very demands of reason which lead us to this idea of God also lead us to abandon it as unintelligible as soon as it is formed. At the final moment of its triumph, reason collapses into mysticism, and is overwhelmed by silence in face of the incomprehensible.

The unintelligibility is obvious. How can there be a being which combines in itself all possible properties, since a very large number of them are incompatible with each other? It is only a verbal sleight of hand to say that what is incompatible on earth will be made compatible in God. Is God supposed to be the heaviest possible being and also the lightest possible being at the same time? Red and blue? Long and short? Hot and cold? No, this is a travesty of the doctrine. But why? Because God is immaterial and contains no material properties; he is pure spirit. There is no escape by this way, however; for now God, who is supposed to contain all properties in himself, turns out to possess no material properties at all. Ah, but may he not contain them in a higher manner? If that means that he may possess a material property which is not material, it is senseless. If it means that he must have the idea (essence or nature) of material things in his mind, then it is clear that matter is only *possible* in God; only the idea of it, which, *qua* idea, is spiritual, actually exists in him. So what happens to the basic principle that causes must be like their effects, from which the whole process of argument began? The whole material world is the effect of a being which is pure spirit; its manifoldness is the effect of a being which is one; its complexity of a being which is simple; its imperfection of a being which is perfect. How much more different can one get?

The whole idea of a 'likeness' between God and creatures collapses when it is explored more fully. Yet it is essential to the construction of a notion of God's perfection which sees it as lying in an enhanced possession of every created property.

In *Summa Theologiae,* qu. 4, art. 3, Thomas distinguishes some different senses of 'likeness' or 'resemblance'. Two things, he says, may share a form of the same type to the same degree; then, like two equally white things, they are exactly alike. Two things may share a form of the same type to different degrees; an example would be two different shades of white. But also, Thomas says, things may share a form, though they are not members of the same species. The example he gives is the sun causing events on earth, and, in general, causal relations between things in different species. This assertion seems to depend solely upon the a priori principle that 'since a thing is active in virtue of its form, its effect must bear a likeness to that form'. That is, the sun must be like its effects, since that is implied in what real causality is. An agent can only do certain sorts of things, which depend upon its own nature, and its effects must in some sense bear the mark of the cause.

Thomas is struggling after the formulation of some principle to rule out the possibility that a cause can produce any effect at all. For if this were the case, the first cause of the world could be of any nature, and no causal argument from the world could enable us to say anything reliable of it. But the concept of resemblance is not well fitted to express this principle, since it is clear that there is no qualitative similarity at all which needs to exist between, say, the sun and the plants of the earth. The case is even more tenuous with God, for he is, according to Thomas, outside any genus. In his case, the likeness can only present 'the sort of analogy that holds between all things because they have existence in common'. Things thus resemble God simply and in so far as they possess existence. Any specific or generic resemblance is now denied, for nothing literally shares a form with God; the similarity is only that both God and creatures exist. Now we have reached a stage when it would be clearer to deny likeness between creatures and God than to continue to affirm it in such an attenuated sense. When one denies any common genus or species, and indeed everything except that both cause and effects exist, one has ceased to say anything at all about God except that he exists. And even that attribution is only made analogically, so it is not too clear either.

One needs to distinguish between the sorts of property which exist in the first cause only as ideas, as possibilities, and the sorts of property which must be actually possessed by that cause itself. In the Thomist conception, this distinction is blurred, because God is said to be absolutely simple. Thus there cannot really be distinct ideas in God; for, if there were, they would be related to each other, but there are no internal relations in a purely simple (non-complex) being. So Aquinas says that relations between the Ideas in God are 'not real relations . . . but relations understood by God' (qu. 15, art. 2). There is not a plurality of ideas in God at all, but only one simple essence, which 'fulfils the definition of an Idea with reference to other things, but not with reference to God himself' (qu. 15, art. 1). Here, the Platonic strain in Thomas's thought comes to the fore, and dominates his concept of God. The eternal Forms, which are the ideas of what anything could possibly be, even before they are made, are more real than the material objects which exemplify them. For they are all in God; and as such, they are all identical with each other, in one indivisible essence. The eternal Ideas are not arbitrarily chosen by God; they necessarily and immutably express his eternal nature, as it is imitable by creatures. What is one and indivisible in God is conceived by us as many and distinct, but in fact the ideas in God are all identical with each other, and with the simple divine essence. God's essence, though simple, is imitable in many partial ways by creatures. One cannot, then, distinguish between possibilities existing in God and properties possessed by God himself; for those possibilities are identical with the one simple essence which is his nature.

The difficulty here is this: the demand that the self-subsistent being should fully explain all other beings seems to lead to the concept of an immutable, fully actual being, like but greater than all its possible effects. The basic principle underlying this inference is that all caused properties must be brought about by something actually like them, and at least as great (since there cannot be more in the effect than in the cause, if one is to be wholly derivable from the other). But the idea of a being which possesses a maximal degree of all possible properties at once seems clearly incoherent. So it follows that the search for a complete rationalistic explanation is doomed to failure.

This leads one to look again at the sort of explanation one is seeking, to see if it can be reformulated without being abandoned. An immediate possibility which suggests itself is that one need not insist that causes actually possess the properties which they bring about in their effects. There is little to support this in experience (hot things do not, as Aristotle thought, have to be caused by hot things), and it would seem to entail that nothing new could ever happen – the whole created world could only be a pale and imperfect reflection of what already exists more fully in God. And that makes the existence of the world very difficult to account for at all. Why should a perfect being produce what can only be less perfect than, and wholly derivative from, itself? There is, of course, a long tradition in rationalist theology which sees the creation as rather unfortunate, as something to be escaped from as soon as possible, by a return to the one source of all. Plotinus, who saw all the universe as emanating necessarily from the perfect being, writes, 'It begins as one, but does not remain one. Unconsciously it becomes multiple, as if pressed down by its own weight. It unfolds itself desirous of becoming all things, although it would have been better for it not to have desired this.' (*Ennead, III,* 8, 8.) The derivation of the world from God, the perfect being, is both unconscious and rather deplorable. The idea of God is quite compatible with the most depressing cosmic pessimism; if only God is perfect, and if the world necessarily derives from him as a less real, refracted image of his being, there need be no notion of purpose and value in the universe at all. Spinoza, who stands in the same sort of tradition, saw no signs of purpose in the universe whatsoever, and found the highest value in the resigned acceptance of necessity. 'All final causes are nothing but human fictions', he says (*Ethics*, pt. 1, appendix).

For this sort of view, there is no reason (in the sense of purpose) for the existence of the world. The only reason is that it derives by necessity from a being which is itself completely perfect. Admittedly, it is rather odd that a being who is, *ex hypothesi*, wholly perfect, should produce an imperfect world. But it must be remembered that the Divine perfection, according to this form of argument, is purely ontological — it is the perfection of possessing the greatest amount of the greatest number of kinds of reality. There is no reason why finite existence, as such, should be desirable. The universe may be wholly necessary, and completely derivative from one self-subsistent being, while being without any purpose or value (in the sense of desirability to any sentient and rational being) whatsoever.

In one way, Spinoza seems to be the only consistent rationalist philosopher. He manages to produce an idea of a self-subsistent being which actually possesses all possible properties by the simple expedient of identifying the universe as a whole with God, and denying that there can be anything possible, over and above what is actual. God, as the all-including and necessary substance, is metaphysically perfect: 'All things are in God, and everything which takes place takes place by the laws alone of the infinite nature of God, and follows . . . from the necessity of his essence (*Ethics*, prop. 16). But, if he avoids the incoherence of positing a simple being who includes all possible properties in himself, he is caught by the difficulty that the self-subsistent being must, by the arguments rehearsed, be immutable, underived and purely actual. If all the things in the universe are changing, contingent and partly potential, how can they form a whole which is immutable, necessary and wholly actual? Spinoza's answer, of course, is that there is only one thing, an absolutely infinite substance 'in itself and conceived through itself' (*Ethics*, def. 3); all finite things are modes or attributes of it. But the contradiction remains: there cannot be an immutable being, all of whose parts change. One must either say that there is an immutable aspect of being, that the universe is immutable in some respects, or that change and complexity are illusions. The latter view is deeply entrenched in the Indian tradition of Sankara, who shares in the cosmic pessimism of this sort of philosophy, holding that the only real wisdom is to overcome illusion and discover one's unity with the Absolute Reality, by ascetic denial of individuality. The former is found in a developed form in the philosophy of Plotinus, who holds that there is an immutable being, 'the One', from which all else necessarily derives.

Taking his cue from Plato's cryptic remarks about the supreme Form of the Good, which, according to the *Republic*, 508, is 'beyond being, surpassing it in dignity and power', Plotinus holds that the supreme principle, the One, 'is not a being because it is precedent of all being' (*Ennead*, VI, 9, 3). Indeed, he goes even further than Plato, saying, 'The One, in its aloneness, can neither know nor be ignorant of anything ... it cannot be called the Good' (*Ennead*, VI, 9, 6). Yet this One is the source of all goodness and being: 'The One produces the second Hypostasis without assent or decree or movement of any kind ... as a radiation that, though it proceeds from the One, leaves its self-identity undisturbed' (*Ennead*, V, 1, 6). The immutability of the One is thus preserved; it does not actually become anything other than it is, yet in some way it overflows into being: 'In order that being be, the One must be not being but being's begetter' (*Ennead*, V, 2, 1).

This overflowing, or emanation, is in no way an act of the One; it just happens, necessarily. Thus one may see the changing universe as one aspect of reality, derivative from the unchanging aspect, which is the One beyond description. It may be thought that the One is beyond description because any attempted description of a metaphysically perfect being would be incoherent. But there is also a form of argument to this conclusion, one rehearsed by Thomas in his proofs of the Divine simplicity. First, God cannot be or have a body, because he is incapable of change and is purely actual; but all material bodies are capable of change and are partly potential. Similarly, God cannot be composed of matter and form, because he is not potential in any respect. Material things are combinations of matter, or 'stuff', and form, which gives them their nature or kind. Individual things participate in forms, and one form can be instantiated in many different instances. God, however, cannot participate in forms, as independent entities, so he cannot be an individual which possesses various properties. He does not, for instance, have the quality of justice 'by participation in the quality of justice', which is something other than himself. So he must himself be the quality of justice; and also he must be goodness, power and so forth. Since everything that exists must exist through sharing in the property of existence, God must be the power of existing *per se*; he must be Existence.

God, the primary existent, is 'a form . . . itself subsisting as a thing . . . not assumed by anything else, and thus individual of itself' (*Summa Theologiae*, qu. 3, art. 2). If one accepts the reality of universal essences, and even their ontological priority over particulars which exemplify them, then God must be a universal and pure Form, the co-inherence of all essences in one indivisible reality. He is not just a being who happens to be the sum of all essences; he is simple, because all complex things depend on their parts, being resolvable into them in principle, whereas God depends upon nothing but himself; so he has no discrete parts. God is identical with his own essence; he does not share it with any other possible being. Further, 'God is not only his own essence, but also his

own existence' (qu. 3, art. 4). He is never potentially existent, since he is never potentially anything. Existence belongs to
his nature; his nature is to exist, in the fullest possible way.

Neither does God belong to a class, since there is no distinction of essence and existence in him. Nor is he a substance, because 'no simple form can be a subject' of predicates
(qu. 3, art. 6). The Thomist notion is of a God who is Abstract Form, a simple being containing all forms, but in a
unique way; for all his properties are identical with each
other, since he contains no parts; 'any one of them is the
same as all the others' (Anselm, *Monologion,* 17). It is at
once apparent that a being who is not a subject or a member
of a class or in any way complex cannot be described by
language which refers to subjects by means of general class-
descriptions, and which consists of many various and complex terms. The problem of analogy assumes the alarming
proportions it does in Thomist theology because God is
defined in such a way that no terms could possibly describe
him. No simple, eternal being can be correctly described in
complex nouns and tensed verbs.

Plotinus attempts to deal with this dilemma by positing
three Hypostases in God. The first, the One, is indescribable,
even by the most general concept of 'being'. It gives rise by
emanation to the second, the Intellect, which 'in its totality
is made up of the Forms' (*Ennead,* V, 9, 8); it is the realm of
possibility, the Platonic world of Ideas. 'In turning towards
itself the One sees. It is this seeing which is Intellect'. (V, 1,
7) Typically, the account is full of logical inconsistencies.
The One is said to be immutable; yet it turns towards itself,
and Intellect is said to be 'its word and deed'. Clearly, the act
of an immutable being must be eternal. That may just be conceivable, but how can the wholly indescribable be said to act,
to see or to be the cause of all?

At times the contradiction comes visibly to the surface.
Dionysius, a Syrian Christian in the Neoplatonic tradition,
writes, 'from its Oneness it becomes manifold while yet

remaining within itself' (*On the Divine Names*, 2, 11); 'It becomes differentiated without loss of undifference'. The picture is presented by Plotinus thus: 'Every nature must produce its next, for each thing must unfold, seedlike, from indivisible principle into a visible effect . . . it must proceed continuously until all things, to the very last, have within the limits of possibility, come forth' (*Ennead*, V, 8, 6). The conceptual difficulty is this: how can the One become without changing? How can it unfold or proceed? If all these distinctions are within the One necessary being, then that being is complex, and we are back to Spinoza's problem. But if they are outside it, how can the simple and ineffable have any effect on the complex and mutable?

The model of emanation suggests an unconscious process, in which the One has no real relation to the world at all. Like a fire which, without intending to, gives heat to the things around it, so the One gives being to the world of multiplicity. But, if the One has no relation to the world, how can the world be said to be produced by it? In Aristotle's metaphysics, the prime mover appears to have no relation to the world, which exists independently of him. But the world is moved by love, or desire, for the prime mover: 'the final cause moves by being loved, while all other things that move do so by being moved' (*Metaphysics*, Λ 7, 1072b). That is one solution to the present difficulty; if matter is given independent existence, it may autonomously strive to imitate the One, without the One paying any attention to or producing effects in it. However, then matter is left as an irrational surd in the cosmology, and one does not escape the theory of a 'world derived from night' which Aristotle derides, the finally inexplicable reality.

The axiom of explicability compels one to attribute the being of matter to the first cause alone. So the primary being brings matter about by a necessary, eternal and unconscious process. The Plotinian Triad, the Divine Being, consists of the wholly simple and ineffable One; the Intellect, identified with the world of Forms; and the third hypostasis, the world-soul, 'the author of all living things . . . it brought order . . . guides . . . gives life and immortality to the world' (*Ennead*, V, 1, 2). Matter itself is a necessary emanation from God, descending gradually towards non-being in every possible degree until at last it vanishes into nothingness.

The Neoplatonic synthesis is immensely ingenious and has had great influence on subsequent Western theology. It unites the concepts of matter, a world-designer, Plato's ineffable form of the Good and the eternal world of Forms in one intelligible system, with the aid of the uniting idea of emanation. All these concepts had been adumbrated in Plato, but had never been brought into any form of systematic unity. They continue to exercise influence on mystical traditions within the Christian churches. But does the system escape the difficulties already raised about the notion of a metaphysically perfect first cause? It may seem to do so, because Plotinus has managed to incorporate the idea of a purposing designer, a being which contains the forms of all possible realities and a simple and purely actual being in the all-inclusive concept of the Divine Triad. But is this more than a verbal conjunction of quite disparate elements?

In the end, I do not think that it is. There is no harm in saying that God is greater than one can conceive, or in saying that there are many things about God which one is quite unable to conceive. But it is ridiculous to say that God is wholly inconceivable, for that would leave the word 'God' without any meaning. There must be some things which are known about God, if we are to use the word intelligibly. The Plotinian tradition stresses the negative way, holding that it is better to say what God is not than what he is. But one cannot be satisfied with wholly negative statements; for that would leave God as a mere nothing. Some versions of the apophatic way seem almost to say as much. Scotus Erigena says, 'The ineffable Nature can be signified by no verb, by no noun and by no other audible sound' (*Periphyseon*, 1, 25). But at least one might say that God is the source of all things. No; in the consistent pursuit of negativity, Erigena goes on: 'True reason completely excludes the category of making from the Divine nature' (1, 98). Where nothing can be said, theism is indistinguishable from atheism.

Plotinus and Dionysius, too, write that God is beyond being and knowing. In Dionysius' words, 'It is the universal cause of existence while itself existing not, for it is beyond all being' (*On the Divine Names*, 1, 1). This is overtly self-contradictory; if there is something which produces being, then there is something, that is, something is, or exists. To try to talk of something existing beyond being is self-refuting. All that can be meant is that God does not exist or know in any way that we can imagine it; but that he exists is a presupposition of saying anything about him at all.

This is plain to the apophatic theologians, and they almost always insist on a cataphatic way, too, by which 'All attributes may be affirmed at once of him' (Dionysius, *On the Divine Names*, 5, 8). One may coin phrases like 'super-essential' or 'super-wise' to speak of God, expressions which are positive in form but negative in meaning. Even so, they are not entirely negative; for ' "It is super-essential' says not what it is but what it is not; for it says that it is not essence but more than essence' (Erigena, *Periphyseon*, 1, 27). That 'more than' adds an important element to sheer negation; it says that it is not inappropriate to call God wise, even though he is more than we conceive by the word 'wise'.

One denies every attribute of God because he is simple; one affirms every attribute of God because he is the cause of all. If the arguments for these conclusions, and the principles on which they are based, are convincing, then one is stuck with the conclusion. But it is hardly an acceptable escape from the incoherence of a wholly ineffable being to add to it the incoherence of a being of whom all attributes can be affirmed at once, and aver that the truth lies in the paradox formed by the combination of two incoherencies.

Thus Plotinus' attempt to preserve Divine simplicity by appeal to an ineffable One, and to preserve Divine omni-causality by appeal to the Intellect, founders. It founders, because what is wholly ineffable cannot be described as the source of all, and because the reification of a world of abstract essences does not guarantee that God contains all realities in himself. If one returns to the basic principles upon which these arguments are founded, one finds that they are two: the principle that the greater cannot come from the less, and the principle that essences are ontologically prior to their instantiations. On closer examination, neither of these prin-ciples is acceptable, as they stand. What is required for a complete explanation of the world is not that the primary being should contain in himself the greatest possible degree of every possible property; that would in fact make the pro-duction of any world an otiose repetition of the already existent. What is required is that things should not come to be from nothing, inexplicably. But this requirement is satis-fied if, in the primary being, one finds, not all actual proper-ties, but the *ideas* of all possible properties together with a principle governing the actualization of some of them. One is not thereby committed to the reification of universals, as independent existents. One is only committed to saying that some actual individual, God, conceives the general patterns of all possible things, as well as bringing some of them, at least, into being. God does not actually have to possess every property. He only needs to possess those properties which are necessary to conceiving all possibles and actualizing some of them: omniscience (knowledge of all possibles) and omni-potence (ability to produce anything possible).

The course of argument which led to conceiving God as the supreme abstract Form, Being-itself, was therefore mis-taken and unnecessary. God, the necessary source of all beings, is logically an individual and a member of the class of 'necessary sources of all beings'. Of course, there can be no other members of that class; but, if classes as such are not objective existents, God does not have to *be* the class or highest universal — self-subsistent existence. He simply has to be an individual which falls under a unique description, and which uniquely could not fail to exist. The Thomist assertion that 'the only genus to which God could belong would be the genus of existent' (qu. 3, art. 5) is incoherent. The class of 'the existent' covers all actual things, not just God. Further, if one tries to speak of the purely, unrestrictedly existent, one ends with the absurdity that there exists something which has no property other than existing, that is, nothing. One can say that God exists by necessity, without being committed to the incoherent assertion that God is identical with 'existence', the emptiest of all categories. One can say that he necessarily possesses various properties, like omnipotence and omniscience, necessity and underivability, without having to say that all those properties are identical with each other, and therefore inconceivable.

In fact, the whole doctrine of Divine simplicity arises from a misinterpretation of the truth that God is not divisible into parts, that all his properties are interconnected. God's properties are necessarily connected in a reciprocally determining whole, and are not just contingently or fortuitously related. The human mind is not well equipped to discern such necessary connections; but we can see in a way how it is that many Divine properties flow from that of aseity or self-determination. However, I can see no a priori reason why the Divine being should not be internally complex, each part depending essentially upon the unity of the whole. Thus one is not compelled to take the step to a wholly ineffable being, so simple that our complex analytic concepts could not grasp it at all. On the contrary, the requirements of rationalism enjoin one to maintain consistently the view that the mind can correctly grasp the nature of God, the primary cause, the complex but unitary reality which explains all others.

If this is thought to be too ambitious, one can only recall that this is the only route that gets one to God in the first place, whether it is admitted or not. So one may as well try to press it home all the way. That is quite compatible with asserting that much of God is beyond rational apprehension; that, indeed, we cannot understand how God knows, or acts, or possesses his being necessarily. But that he does, we may correctly assert, and to that extent we may truly know what God is.

What is left, then, of the traditional arguments for a metaphysically perfect being? All the Platonic arguments that causes must be like but greater than their effects must be abandoned. All experience suggests that effects can be very different from their causes, and I do not see how a theist can avoid saying at least that the material universe is very different from the immaterial God, its cause. What remains is that, if the world is to be intelligible, effects must be explicable from their causes; and that, ultimately, means that there must be archetypal patterns of possible effects and laws of transformation, in the originative being. Reference to these archetypes can provide a complete explanation of all that comes to be, together with the provision of a reason why some rather than others are actualized. We have in this chapter considered as a reason for actualization only the emanationist theory – that all effects follow necessarily from the first cause. So the first cause needs to be a container of archetypes, a 'place of Forms'; and as such, it is conceivable as a Mind, though very different from human minds.

As the Mind which is the source of all possibles, and thereby of all actuals, God is unlimited in power and knowledge by anything outside himself. Nothing is possible that he does not know; nothing can become actual that he does not bring about. Being immutable, he cannot change or develop; being necessary, no similar being could be better than he. It is accordingly senseless to speak of God as imperfect; though, I have suggested, it is incoherent to speak of him as perfect, in the sense of actually possessing in higher manner all possible properties. All attempts to develop such a notion have failed, from Sankara to Spinoza, from Plotinus to Aquinas. All of them entail denying that God is an individual; he becomes either the whole of reality (Spinoza), the completely ineffable (Sankara) or an abstract pure Form (Aquinas). Whereas what the intelligibility argument requires is an individual which is necessary, immutable, omniscient and omnipotent cause of all things.

Once one abandons the Platonic principle that essences are ontologically prior to individuals, that possibles are more real than actuals, there is no longer any compelling reason for taking God to be the Supreme Essence. Rather, one is free to conceive him as the uniquely self-existent individual, containing all possibles in his own being (and so being 'complete' in the sense that all possible reality is exhaustively specified in him), and being immutable and necessarily existent. These five properties of aseity, necessity, unity, immutability and completeness are what may be called the metaphysical perfections of the Divine being. But the consideration has also been introduced that God is conceivable on the analogy of a cosmic mind, in some sense omnipotent and omniscient. Such attributes as these are certainly part of the traditional idea of God. We have seen that, on the emanationist view, the universe flows from God by some sort of rational necessity. This is not, however, the view that has found favour in the Christian tradition of theism. There, the doctrine of creation has been preferred. The reasons for this, and the difficulty of formulating a consistent concept of a perfect creator, must now be explored.

4   Creation

The view that everything that exists in the material world is a necessary emanation from one necessary immutable being is one that tends to reinforce a generally mystical approach to the religious life. This approach is developed most notably in the Vedantic and Buddhist traditions of India, but it is found in the West in a persistent undercurrent of Neoplatonist thought. When the theory dominates, one will tend to interpret the supreme being, not as an active spiritual force, but as an immutable reality which the mind can contemplate. The aim of the spiritual life is consequently often seen as the mind's own attainment of the clear vision of the nature of the real. Brahman or Nirvana are themselves immutable, and thus cannot actively relate to men. They are the grounds of possibility, not external to the world, but enveloping and containing it. The spiritual goal is naturally conceived as a coming to perceive how things really are, in their dependence on the real; there is no change in Brahman, so the power of grace is the intrinsic attraction of the Ideal. If, in this tradition, one seems to find more active senses of liberating power, they will have to be attributed to the gods, devas or saints, who stand on a lower level than Brahman itself. So active polytheism often co-exists with the deeper quest to open the mind to the knowledge of absolute reality, of which we are parts, or necessary implications.

Apprehensions of God will be interpreted in terms of union or absorption, the merging in a wider whole rather than as interpersonal fellowship with a supreme spiritual and personal being. Providence will be interpreted in terms of necessary laws governing human action, like laws of necessary moral cause and effect, or *karma,* rather than as personal patternings of experience. And moral perceptions may be construed as apprehensions of immutable Ideas, drawing one towards union with them, as exemplary patterns of life. Both in Indian and Western traditions, these interpretations also express a generally ascetic attitude to the world. But this seems to be because of the belief that existence is a fall from the immutably perfect into isolation and individuation. Since the truly real is inactive, unchanging, the ideal of life is to become so too. No positive value can be put on the creative process of change itself, since all is a necessary expression of a changeless being. There can be no radically new goals, and all is in order as it is. The goal of life is the return to the changeless origin, the perfect, from which all finite existence is a refracted degeneration.

There have been attempts to express a less ascetic attitude to a generally emanationist universe. The Stoics, for example, found a positive value in the existence of finite reality. But even then, the universe itself has no inner purpose or goal: 'the cycles of the universe are ever the same, above and below, from age to age' (M. Aurelius, *Meditations,* 9, 28). The world as a whole is entirely perfect, but providence is directed only to the good of the whole, not the parts: 'The gods take care of great things, and disregard the small' (Cicero, *The Nature of the Gods,* 2, 66). Resigned acceptance may be considered an appropriate attitude to the permanent, endless and necessary flux; but so may resentment at being an insignificant cog in the production of what is in the end a form of magnified egoism, the self-preservation of the cosmic whole.

This whole view of God as the immutable individual which includes all finite reality within itself (since the finite is a necessary, eternal and immutable emanation from it) has arisen from the pursuit of the goal of total intelligibility. But there are difficulties with it, when applied as a model to explain the actual universe. One is the point noticed by Kant when he stated that the quest for total intelligibility was indeed a demand of reason, but that it could never be objectively verified; it is possible, after all, that the world is not totally intelligible, at least not in the sense that we conceive of such intelligibility. One must be aware that, though the canons of reason may fit the universe adequately, they may not; the sense of mystery, deeply rooted in the religious consciousness, must place a permanent question mark against all our attempts to comprehend in some final systematic way the nature of ultimate reality. Mystery should never be used as an escape from asking the hard questions, but it must be placed against the final strivings of reason when it reaches its limits, to remind us that we can never be sure that we have correctly grasped the truth we seek. Indeed, with Kant himself, we can go further, and say that the chequered career of metaphysics, the apparently irresolvable disputes of its practitioners, and the antinomies and paradoxes into which reason perpetually falls, seem to point to a deep impossibility of arriving at final systematic truth about the ultimate nature of things by reason alone.

Such insights cannot lead us to abandon reason, our only guardian against intellectual chaos. It is only the rational pursuit of intelligibility which leads to the formation of that concept of God which can be the adequate object of our worship. But they can lead us not to neglect other considerations, also deeply rooted in human nature, but not subject to complete rational clarification — considerations of morality and practical commitment, for example, and of faith and love. It is when one turns to examine such things that the rationalist model seems too systematic and complete to fit reality as we experience it. The inescapable facts of evil and freedom, of creative purpose, human autonomy and the dilemmas of choice place a huge question mark over any assertion that the world as a whole is a totally intelligible system. One can see this reaction to rationalism very clearly in the course of European philosophy after Hegel, who was interpreted, whether fairly or not, as a supreme rationalist, deriving the whole process of world history from the necessities of absolute spirit.

Almost as soon as the great systems of idealist rationalism were constructed, they disappeared from the scene, as if suffocated by their own over-rich vocabulary, unrestrained speculation and sheer ontological greediness. One can be carried away by the heady mixture, the feeling that the rationality of the real is being disclosed to the initiated, for just so long. Then the sense of reality steps in, and with the first sceptical doubt, the vast systems crumble silently away. Thus in face of the cosmic optimism of Hegel, who was bound to see the worst evil and suffering as a necessary part of a truly rational whole, the stark pessimism of Schopenhauer could only construe the Will which expresses itself in the world as purposeless, doomed to frustration and bound to a wheel of endless sorrow. In face of the reification of the abstract Idea, as the foundation of reality, the materialism of Feuerbach and Engels stressed the primacy of the concrete, the here and now. And in face of the assertion of the omnipresence of Reason in the world, the existentialism of Kierkegaard defended the place of the irrational, the sheerly contingent, the absolutely free and unique personal existence of each human individual. In the end, it is just too much to suggest that the real is the rational, and the rational is the real, in a world where evil, freedom, contingency and uniqueness play such a very obvious part.

The intellectual weakness of rationalism lies precisely in its claim to an intellectual strength, which can only be bought at the price of overlooking all recalcitrant material which does not fit into the speculative scheme. The moral weakness of rationalism is its implicit justification of everything that actually exists. The iron necessities and rational determinations of history lead all too easily to a loss of moral sensibility, of the resolution to oppose evil wherever it is found, however necessary pure speculation may suppose it to be. Just as the total transcendence of the Thomist God who is abstract Form leaves everything in the world basically unimportant — since nothing can change or affect the only true reality — so the total immanence of the God who is the all-inclusive Spirit leaves everything in the world uncriticizable — since it expresses what the only true reality, perfect as a whole, necessarily is.

It may be thought that this comment is unfair both to the idealist tradition of Hegel and to the Christian tradition of Aquinas. Both of these traditions oppose the unlimited or infinite being of the Absolute to the dependent and finite beings of the world, even though they develop apparently quite different notions of infinity. Aquinas follows the Aristotelian tradition of distinguishing the infinite sharply from the finite, since what is completely unlimited cannot even be internally limited, and thus cannot contain any finite element at all. Thereby arises the doctrine of Divine simplicity, and with it the total separation of God from the world. 'Nothing can come into contact with God or partially intermingle with him in any way.' (*Summa Theologiae,* qu. 3, art. 8) So it is true that nothing can change or affect God in any way. Aristotle's prime mover was so self-sufficient that he did not know or create the world, but remained eternally bound up in the contemplation of his own perfection, as the *noesis noeseos,* the thinker whose object of thought is his own being. Aquinas's *Actus Purus,* however, in accordance with Christian doctrine, both creates and knows perfectly the finite world. And this doctrine of free, intended creation may seem to give Aquinas an escape route from pure rationalism.

Similarly, Hegel stands in the Plotinian tradition of including the finite within the infinite, since what is completely unlimited cannot be limited by any reality outside itself, and thus it must contain every possible reality within its own being. Thereby arises the doctrine of the Divine all-inclusiveness, and with it the total identification of God with the world. 'Reason is consciously aware of itself as its own world, and of the world as itself' (*The Phenomenology of Mind*, ch. 6, p. 457). So it is true that everything in the world expresses what Absolute Spirit eternally is. Plotinus' Divine Triad gave rise to the world by absolute necessity, so that everything must necessarily be what it is; the grip of rationalism remains firm. Hegel's Absolute Spirit, however, exhibits a form of dialectical dynamism which makes it unclear just how far real contingency could enter into the system, and loosen the grip a little.

For both these traditions, which between them have dominated Western thought about the nature of God, the primary problem is that of taking account both of the rationality of the real, which alone can license belief in one self-determining reality, and of the contingency of the finite. The Greek solution, or rather avoidance of the problem, is quite unsatisfactory. It simply opposes a wholly rational realm of Forms or prime mover to a wholly contingent and everlasting matter, and thus simply succeeds in undermining the rational basis of the real altogether. If the primary reality is indeed immutable and eternal (since what is in principle incapable of change must be timeless, time being the form of change) then the theory of emanation seems most natural. But if that is the theory that all finite beings flow by timeless necessity from the infinite, then the contingency of the finite is undermined.

The conceptual breakthrough that the Christian faith offered to the resolution of the problem was the doctrine of creation *ex nihilo*. According to this doctrine, matter does not exist independently of God; it is brought into being solely by Divine power. Before it existed, there was simply nothing material at all, though there was always God. Aquinas noted, quite correctly, that this does not entail that the world had a beginning in time, or that it will have an end in time. The world may always have existed; all that is necessary is that it should depend solely and at every moment upon the power of God for its being, whereas God depends upon nothing, but is self-determining. So far, there is no distinction in principle from the theory of emanation. But there is an important second part to the doctrine: namely, that creation is a free act, performed through intellect and will. The world does not just come into being unconsciously; it is willed by God, who desires that it should exist, who chooses to bring it into being. Without this element of free choice, there would be no creation, no making, but only unconscious generation.

The idea of creation does seem to allow contingency to the world. One imagines a being surveying all possibilities, not being compelled to actualize any one set, but deciding by undetermined choice to actualize some of them. The only reason for the existence of that world will lie in the undetermined choice of the creator, and since the choice is undetermined, the world will be truly contingent — it could have been otherwise. Yet a measure of intelligibility will be preserved, for the choice will be a rational one, made in fully knowledge of all consequences and alternatives, by a necessary and self-determining being.

The outlook seems hopeful. And yet those philosophers who have tried to work out a coherent doctrine of creation have run into enormous difficulties, upon which their attempts have mostly foundered. First of all, if God really is self-sufficient, as the axiom of intelligibility seems to require him to be, how can it come about that he creates a world at all? It seems an arbitrary and pointless exercise. On the other hand, if God really is a necessary and immutable being, how can he ever have a free choice; surely all that he does will have to be done of necessity and without any possibility of alteration? The old dilemma — either God's acts are necessary and therefore not free (could not be otherwise), or they are free and therefore arbitrary (nothing determines what they shall be) — has been sufficient to impale the vast majority of Christian philosophers down the ages.

Leibniz's doctrine is well known: God sees all possible worlds in knowing his own eternal being, and he chooses to bring into being that which is best, in accordance with the principle of perfection. God, being what he is, must choose the best of all possible worlds; he cannot fail to bring it about. So he is free only in that he acts in accordance with his own intellectual perception. In an essay 'On the Ultimate Origin of Things' (1697) Leibniz writes that 'there is in things that are possible . . . a certain need for existence, or . . . a claim to exist . . . essence in itself tends towards existence'. The world, as it were, presses into existence, and the world which succeeds in existing is that one 'by whose means the greatest possible amount of essence or possibility is brought into existence'. The world is not metaphysically necessary, in that its essence does not involve existence, but it is morally necessary: 'it is determined in such a way that its contrary would imply imperfection or moral absurdity'. In the end, the world must be what it is, if God is what he necessarily is. Once again, rationalist necessitarianism has triumphed, and real contingency disappears.

Aquinas explicitly rejects the argument that God must create the best of all possible worlds, on the ground that the concept of a best possible world is not coherent. There could always be a world better in some respects than any actual world. Just as it makes no sense to talk of a most beautiful possible painting — though some paintings are definitely more beautiful than others — so it makes no sense to talk of a best possible world. One might think, then, that Thomas is better able to escape necessitarianism, for there is a range of possible worlds, of all of which it is true that it is good for them to exist, between which God can freely choose. However, the difficulties Thomas faces arise from the doctrines of immutability, simplicity and necessity, to which the axiom of intelligibility seems to have led. Briefly put, if God is simple, he contains no parts or internal divisions. So, if he is necessary, he is wholly necessary, and can contain no part which is not necessary. Thus, whatever God does, he does by necessity of his nature. Once again, we arrive at the position that God has no alternatives open in creating the world. God may be said to will the existence of the world simply by his own will and pleasure. But, since that will and pleasure belong to a simple and necessary being, there is really nothing else that he can do. Creation is necessary to such a God; and this, despite Thomas's affirmation, following Christian dogma, that God need not have created the world, but could have continued to exist solely on his own, as self-sufficient.

Plotinus denied creation precisely because a free act of creation would entail change in God. For, if God could either create a world or not create a world, then there must be a state of God in which he has not yet decided which to do. The doctrine that he eternally (timelessly) and immutably decides in favour of one case is incoherent, for there can be no preceding state of God in which he decides. So the idea of a decision is vacuous; he just is in one state or the other, and nothing determines which, except his own concept. It is perhaps possible that a concept may allow God to be either in state A or in state B; if so, the actualization of one or other state must be random, left undetermined by anything. Whereas the concept of free decision implies that whichever state God is in is not undetermined or random; it is caused by a choice which could have been otherwise. The choosing must precede the existence of the state in question. So God must be conceived as changing from a state in which he has not yet decided to a state in which the decision to actualize one state has been taken. So, Plotinus concludes, since God is immutable, creation cannot be a free act of God.

The admission of freedom into the universe is the downfall of sufficient causality. It entails that there are states not sufficiently determined by anything. They are, however, not completely uncaused, for they are brought into being by a mental act, which is partly guided by an envisaged idea of a goal, and partly impelled by open-ended creative impulse.

One may think of the way in which an artist has some idea of what he wants to create. He has materials to work on and past examples and training to guide his activity, so it is not blind or irrational or arbitrary. Yet a large part of the attraction and interest of what he produces is due to his unique originality, which both develops from his past aims and actions and also advances in new and unpredictable ways to unforeseen actualizations of the creative idea.

One may think that creativity of this sort is a fundamental value, which could not exist in a sufficiently determined universe, but which is intrinsically worthwhile. One of the main characteristics of personal being is dynamic and creative activity, always moving on to new self-chosen goals. A condition of such a characteristic is the existence of a form of forward-looking or purposive causality which is not sufficiently determining, but is genuinely and radically creative. But such a notion of creative activity is essentially temporal; the agent grows and develops in his own creative action, and unfolds the archetypal ideas in unpredictable actualizations and concretions. It is also essentially contingent, for a creative action could have taken many diverse forms, and none of them follow of necessity from their antecedents. One understands the intelligibility of the universe, not on the model of a mathematical deduction from necessary axioms, but on the model of a purposive exercise of free creativity, unfolding in contingent ways the implications of archetypal ideas.

Such a model of creative causality clearly coheres with the idea of the great designer, or archetypal and purposive causality suggested by the various forms of the argument from design or purpose in the universe. But it seems to require a temporal, contingent God, and for that reason it has failed to satisfy the demands of reason and the religious consciousness for a secure and inexponable basis for the rationality, beauty and moral purpose of the universe. In traditional Christian theology, the axiom of intelligibility prevailed; and so the suggestion of a truly creative God was never properly developed. One can see in the work of Aquinas the way in which free creation is at once asserted and qualified out of existence by the demands of the concepts of necessity, simplicity and eternity in the Divine nature.

Thomas starts his exposition of the doctrine of creation from the unpromising premiss that 'nothing outside himself is God's aim' (*Summa Theologiae*, qu. 19, art. 1). This follows from the complete self-sufficiency of God; there can be nothing outside himself which he needs or desires. Indeed, 'the relations that God is said to bear to creatures . . . really exist not in God but in the creatures' (qu. 6, art. 2), so God cannot even be related to anything outside himself, in knowledge or action. That is because any relation in God would have to be part of the Divine essence; yet that essence is simple and contains no relations, and God is not related to the world by necessity, which would make him dependent upon it in some way. This doctrine is wholly unacceptable; it is analytically true that, if I am related by relation r to God, then he is related by some cognate relation to me; and any view which issues in a denial of this logical truth must be mistaken. But it is symptomatic of the strains Thomas is prepared to put on logic in order to preserve the simple infinity of the Divine being (which, of course, as I have held, there is not much reason to preserve).

Yet Thomas can hardly escape from the fact that God does create a world. So, he says, God 'wills his own being and the being of others', since 'it befits the divine goodness that others also should partake of it' (qu. 19, art. 2). 'As he understands things other than himself in understanding his own being, so likewise he wills them in willing his own goodness.' This seems clearly to entail the necessity of the created world, since God's will is identical with his essence. Yet Thomas still wants to say that things 'add no fulfilment to him, there is no absolute need for him to will them' (qu. 19, art. 3). If God wills x contingently, then he can only know that x exists contingently (he cannot know necessarily what could have been otherwise). Yet 'Whatever God knows he knows of necessity', because 'in him intellect and what is known must be identical in every way' (qu. 14, art. 2).

God cannot be dependent for his knowledge on anything outside himself; for again, that would undermine his self-sufficiency. It follows immediately that 'things other than himself he seees not in themselves but in himself, because his essence contains the likeness of things other than himself' (qu. 14, art. 5). In fact, since all God's perfections are identical with each other and with his essence, his knowledge is identical with his will. So Thomas can say, 'God's knowledge is prior to natural things' (qu. 14, art. 8); there can be no events in the world which really could be other than they are, since God's knowledge of them is immutable and necessary, and defines their very existence. It is, in short, impossible to see how the doctrine that God must know and will the world simply in the same act as knowing and willing himself, as a necessary, eternal being, can be reconciled with the assertion of genuine contingency (that x might have been other than it is, given that God remains the same in all essential respects) in the world.

This failure has fairly drastic consequences for the doctrines of human freedom and destiny, which Thomas does not hesitate to draw. Since 'by one act God wills everything in his goodness' (qu. 19, art. 6), he wills the world as a complete whole in one indivisible act. He cannot therefore await the unpredictable decisions of creatures, before deciding what is to happen next. He must see their end at their beginning, and, like Leibniz's God, choose a complete possible world, without any motive for doing so other than his own fiat. 'The plan of predestination is certain, though the freedom of choice . . . is not abolished' (qu. 23, art. 6). But such freedom is in fact a mockery. God 'does not will to some the blessing of eternal life' (qu. 23, art. 3); moreover, 'the foreknowledge of merit is not the motive or reason of predestination'. 'Why does he choose some to glory while others he rejects? His so willing is the sole ground' (qu. 23, art. 5). So God knows the precise individuals who will be saved (a minority, Thomas thinks) and determines that they will be saved; only then does he so arrange proximate causes (prayers and good works) which appear to bring salvation about. We appear to be saved by our faith, but that faith itself is implanted by God, as a proximate cause of the salvation which he infallibly wills. Although Thomas speaks of contingency in the world, it is clear that what he means is that proximate causes are contingent — considered in themselves, they do not entail their effects. Still, all that happens is determined solely by God himself.

Some of the moral distastefulness of this view might be removed by adopting the theory that all men, not just a minority, will be saved from eternal suffering. But even then, the whole nature of every individual, with all its acts and intentions, is willed solely by God, so that any real doctrine of personal responsibility is in danger of being undermined. It is interesting to see how, in the Islamic tradition, a stress on the total omnipotence of God has led to the development of forms of pantheism in Sufi mysticism. Where God alone determines everything by his pure will, human choices easily come to be seen as the choices of God himself, through men. Then, of course, the problem of moral evil, of suffering and ignorance and misplaced desire, becomes enormous. To allow for moral freedom, irrationality and ignorance, one needs to distinguish sharply between the efficient causes of evil and God himself, while yet one cannot allow the Divine originative causality to be undermined. Thereby arises one of the central dilemmas of theism; and it cannot be said that Thomas's efforts to reconcile human freedom with Divine causality are successful. For the Divine act of creation is timeless and changeless, and thus unaffected by what it creates. There is accordingly no place for a real efficient causality other than God's, which may modify his knowledge or responsive action.

The basic metaphysical difficulty of Thomas's view of creation is that a God who is wholly necessary is supposed to create a world which there was no necessity for him to create, and in which there is real contingency, freedom and evil and ignorance. The doctrine of creation differs from that of emanation only in that in the former God brings things about through free rational choice, whereas in the latter he does so by unconscious necessity. But what notion of choice is really applicable to a necessary and simple being? One envisages God first looking at all possibilities, and then deciding which to actualize. But there are two fatal conceptual difficulties with this picture. Being wholly necessary, God cannot do anything other than he does, and being purely actual, he actually is all that he could ever be, and so could not possibly be otherwise. So freedom disappears. Secondly, being simple, God cannot do one thing after another, so his envisaging and his creating must be one indivisible act; his choice of an actual world is not caused by some preceding, undecided, state of himself. But if, for God to conceive possibles is the same act as for him to create this world, then the difference between emanation and creation collapses. As his conception of all possibles is uncaused, being part of his underived nature, so his bringing about of this world must be uncaused, being the same act. So one cannot really say that the act of creation was caused by an act of contingent choice. God's bringing about of this world follows directly from his nature, and so collapses into a form of emanation, in which the Divine knowledge can play no real causal role, since it can make no difference to an act which must be completely uncaused.

In Thomism, the contingency of the world must ultimately disappear, and to that extent it undermines the distinctive contribution which the notion of creation could make to an understanding of the intelligibility of nature. The view has the merit of making it clear, once and for all, that if the world is to be contingent, and man really free, contingency and mutability must exist within God himself. This certainly runs counter to traditional doctrines of God, and it seems to conflict with the axiom of intelligibility. It is possible, however — and I think it is in fact the case — that there is a way of avoiding that conflict, that the discovery of it adds a significant additional element to the comprehensibility and explanatory value of theism and that the traditional doctrines arise from the failure to perceive it. For the moment, in the hope that such a way will prove convincing, I want to explore the concept of creation a little further, on the assumption that change and complexity can be properly ascribed to God.

The basic notion which has controlled the development of traditional doctrines of God is the notion of self-sufficiency. The primary, all-explaining being must be self-sufficient, since it must be wholly self-explanatory. The difficulty which arises at once is that though the self-sufficient being is postulated precisely in order to account for the existence of the finite, changing and complex entities of the universe, once one has a self-sufficient being, the existence of anything other than it seems to be unnecessary and superfluous. If God is distinguished from the world, opposed to it as simple to complex, eternal to temporal, immutable to changing and infinite to finite, then as we have just seen it is extremely difficult to see how such a God can be related to the world at all. But if God is said to include the world in his own being, either by identity or emanation, it is equally difficult to see how there can be any freedom or contingency in the universe.

The way out of this impasse is to reject the doctrine of Divine self-sufficiency. One may continue to say that God is uniquely self-determining and unlimited by anything that he does not originate himself. There is nothing that exists that is not either part of God or created wholly by God. This preserves the necessary element of Divine primacy of being, but involves a rejection of the view that God is the supreme case of self-centred egoism, the Aristotelian *noesis noeseos*, finding supreme happiness in self-contemplation, a sort of eternal Narcissist. But I should stress here again that this is only objectionable if there *is* anything else that God could contemplate. One may find a deeper clue to the nature of the Divine in the statement that 'he who seeks to save himself must lose himself' (Matt. 16: 25); that the perfection of the Divine nature lies, not in its infinite self-satisfaction, but in its self-giving love.

Of course, there is nothing other than God and independent of him to which he can give himself. But may not God bring into being that which, being other than him though always wholly dependent upon him, can be the object of his love and sharer, by participation, in his own nature? Some have held that, if an almighty God brings anything into being, he must also determine its every act and thought, that Divine omnipotence is incompatible with created freedom. Even those who would reject rationalism completely in their general philosophy, lapse into it when thinking about God, and insist on things they would otherwise wholly deny. Why should an almighty being not allow real freedom and independence to creatures, on condition that their power is finite and could be annihilated at any time by him?

If freedom, in the sense of acts not sufficiently caused but brought about by creative choice, is possible at all, then clearly God cannot logically sufficiently cause any free act of a creature. But he can sufficiently cause the existence of a creature which is capable of such free acts; and he can set the limits, the alternatives between which such freedom operates. Now if God himself acts freely, such action is possible. Thus, if God is free and almighty, he can bring into being creatures which are free, and therefore not sufficiently determined in all their acts by him or anything else. No doubt he could also create beings which are not free in that sense; he is free to do that. But the advantage of creating free beings is that they are thereby nearer to the Divine nature, and can respond to God's love and interact with him in a way not possible to necessitated beings.

It may still be objected that a granting of real freedom to creatures may involve a thwarting of God's purposes, since creatures may not do what God wants them to do. They will accordingly limit his power, and it will no longer be true that 'God's will inevitably is always fulfilled' (*Summa Theologiae*, qu. 19, art. 6). That is so; but is easily coped with by using the very traditional distinction between Divine intentions and permissions. Whatever God intends inevitably comes about. But even God cannot intend on behalf of another rational creature; he can hope, wish or desire. And those hopes not only can be, but are constantly thwarted; that is precisely the import of moral evil and sin. The whole idea of creation as a form of Divine self-giving, a love which goes out of itself to a freely responsive object, entails that God puts himself at the disposal of creatures, and limits himself in relation to them. But all that happens does so by Divine permission, and what that says is that God could at any time destroy or modify the world he has made. What he could not do is both to create a universe of free creatures and at the same time ensure that they always did what he wanted.

Another possible objection is that God could not possibly create beings which are other than himself. For Hegel the point would be that God, as infinite, must include everything in his own being; for Aquinas, it is impossible for any being other than God to influence him in any way, and thus to have any real independence. In speaking of creation, it must be clear that one is not saying that God and the world are distinct substances in the same sense, standing over against each other, excluding each other like two blocks of wood in empty space. As Augustine puts it, 'God is both interior to everything because all things are in him and exterior to everything because he is above all things' (*De Genesi ad litteram liber imperfectus*, 8, 26, 48). I can never be outside God; for he knows me directly and can cause me to cease to be at any moment; I exist only by his presence and power. God must be conceived as having direct knowledge of every created thing and the ability to act directly, in an unmediated way, on any created thing. This is the traditional doctrine of Divine omnipresence; and it can be pictorially expressed by saying that the world is the body of God, a doctrine very central to the Vedantic philosophy of Ramanuja. But that picture is inadequate in many ways; for God is not limited by this 'body', since it depends wholly upon his will, and does not grow or fail like human bodies; and God is more present to each thing even than the soul is to a human body. Nevertheless, one may say that the universe is part of God, as long as it is seen to be contingent and wholy dependent upon his will.

For Aquinas, then, there is a sense in which the world is interior to God, as directly willed and known by him. And for Hegel, there is a sense in which the world is other than God, as a community of finite spirits freely choosing good or evil, yet shaped by the grand design of Absolute Spirit into an inevitable final destiny. Both authors realize the futility of making an over-simple distinction between identity and otherness in regard to God, yet neither is able to overcome the inherent limitations imposed by their common belief in the self-sufficiency of the Divine. If one abandons that concept, there is no reason why God should not bring into being agents which freely decide their own futures and which are distinct subjects of awareness, with unique viewpoints. These agents never become independent of God, they are not necessary to his being God and even taken all together they by no means exhaust the reality of God. It is only by his creating and sustaining action that they exist at all, and he is present to them in action and knowledge much more intimately than the mind is present in any human body.

Creation is thus in one sense a self-limitation of God. His power is limited by the existence of beings, however limited, with power to oppose him. His knowledge is limited by the freedom of creatures to actualize genuinely new states of affairs, unknown by him until they happen. His beatitude is limited by the suffering involved in creaturely existence. But in another sense, creation is a vast extension of the sorts of goods that exist, and of the sorts of perfection that God himself possesses. If there is no creation, then there can be no pursuit of creative activity by God, no delighting in the being of creatures and their happiness, no sharing of the Divine goodness with others, and no object upon which God's love could be centred. The basic reason for creation is that it brings about forms of goodness and value which otherwise would not exist. In brief, it makes it possible for God to be a God of love, possessing the properties of creativity, appreciative knowledge and sharing communion, which are the highest perfections of personal being.

It may seem, then, that God, in order to be what he is, must create some world of finite beings, containing centres of awareness which can share in his life. There is no necessity for him to create this particular world, nor is it necessary that he should create any world at all. But if he is to be a loving being, limiting himself in order to pursue new values of creativity and community, then he cannot remain, like the Aristotelian and Thomist Gods, satisfied with the eternal contemplation of his own perfection. The static Greek idea of perfection as necessarily changeless — since any change must be for the worse — is decisively replaced by the dynamic idea of perfection as creative, and therefore changing. The central Christian affirmation that 'God is love' (1 John 4: 16), and the revelation of the Divine character on the cross as self-giving, suffering and thereby achieving glory, both support this replacement. It is in fact extraordinary that Christian theologians should have been so mesmerized by Greek concepts of perfection that they have been unable to develop a more truly Christian idea of the God whose revealed nature is love.

One cannot say that God must necessarily create some world, on pain of failure to be God. But one can say that God can only determine his own being as self-giving love if he both creates and responsively relates to some world. And, given that he has done so, it is a mistake to try to preserve an idea of Divine self-sufficiency, by denying that he depends upon any finite thing in any way. For that would entail a denial that the Divine nature can be co-operative, self-giving love.

Some philosophers have tried to show that God could express self-giving love even without creation, by positing a sort of committee of gods, loving each other. Only McTaggart really appears to have taken this suggestion seriously, and he accepted that this was hardly a form of theism at all. If there can be only one self-determining being, the hypothesis is ruled out as incoherent anyway. Others have suggested that the Trinity is a sort of social reality, that there are three persons (centres of awareness) in one substance. But, in addition to the fact that this conflicts with all traditional views of the Trinity, it is clear that a person is a substance, and that it is one being who is omnipotent, not a society of persons. To admit many centres of awareness in God would split the Divine being unacceptably, entailing that none of them was omniscient or omnipotent. The view is indistinguishable from a more robust polytheism, and must be rejected by thoroughgoing monotheists, such as Christians are supposed to be.

If one cannot be content with a society of gods, or a God who is some sort of society, the only alternative seems to be that the one and only God must freely bring into being other centres of awareness, which can be given such a degree of autonomy as is necessary for them to constitute, with God, a society of interacting personal beings. We can thus say that, if and in so far as 'self-giving love' is an essential characterization of God, he must create some finite world. Though such a world will limit his being in certain ways, it will also extend it in other ways. The limitations will always be self-created and the Divine dependence upon the world will always be such that God wills it and could revoke it at any time, so that neither denigrates from the primacy and perfection of God.

If 'self-giving love' is not an essential property of God, but simply one uniquely valuable but contingent expression of his nature, which is not necessarily actualized, then one will not be able to infer the necessity of creation; God might always have been the self-contemplating intellect conceived by Aristotle. Nevertheless, the world does exist, and, in relation to it, God is the truly creative, changing and responsive being which the Bible, but, oddly enough, not traditional theology, has taken him to be.

It is the notion of a creator God which is the distinctive contribution of Christian revelation (though not Christian theology) to rational theism, and which resolves the residual problems of the Greek conception of the Divine in its relation to the world. The elegant synthesis of Plotinus left contingency and freedom impossible. The remorseless logic of Aquinas left the prime mover incapable of real relation to the world. By a rejection of the basic doctrine of self-sufficiency one can move to the idea of a truly creative being, which can freely choose to bring about subjects of awareness other than himself, and thereby actualize new forms of value which would not otherwise exist. It is then possible to take a much more positive view of the finite world, as purposively created to express forms of positive goodness; and the creative and communal pursuit of freely chosen goals becomes a primary value rooted in the nature of the creator himself. And it is possible to give freedom and responsibility a fundamental place in one's view of reality, and to admit a form of personal relationship to God in prayer which is impossible with the immutable, impassable God of Thomism.

In analysing the traditional notion of Divine perfection as the possession of all possible properties maximally, I suggested that the element of truth in this notion could best be preserved by conceiving of God as a sort of cosmic mind, containing all possibles as its ideas; this was, in essence, the Augustinian revision of Platonism. The idea of a Divine mind fits very well with the idea of a creator, working through freedom to realize constantly developing purposes. But one may go further, and suggest that a coherent idea of a perfect being can only be developed when a notion of purposive causality has been articulated, which will reveal the concept of intrinsic value, which must be part of the idea of the perfect being. The ideas of a Divine mind, and of the intrinsic values which a perfect being must possess, may both be elaborated by a study of purposive causality in the world, of what is traditionally called 'the design argument'. We shall then be able to see more clearly what a perfect Divine mind would be; and will finally see how, and in what sense, it can be identified with the eternal and self-existent source of all being which the arguments from intelligibility lead one to postulate.

5   Purpose

When God is said to be the creator of everything other than himself, he is conceived as bringing the universe into being for a purpose, which he freely chooses. The universe will therefore exhibit not only a structure of rational, law-like necessity, but will also reveal signs of purpose and value. So one must ask whether such signs can be discerned, and, if they can, what sort of being they suggest as their cause. In this way, I aim to show that the doctrine of creation is more explanatory of the nature of the world than the doctrine of emanation, and to elaborate on the idea of a perfect being by introducing the idea of the personal perfections which such a being must possess.

When one asks whether there are signs of purpose in nature, one is asking whether one of the basic, irreducible explanatory principles in terms of which one understands the world must be that of purposive causality. In asking about purpose, one wants to know if there is an end-state which will put certain sequences of events before it into perspective, as means to achieving it. A purposive process is a process culminating in a valued state, a state for the sake of which other states might be taken to exist. Nor may the valued state result by accident, like the lucky throw of a die which brings a fortune. For purpose to exist, the process must be directed to producing the value, must be aimed at it. Thus one only properly understands what is going on when one sees the end to which the process is directed, or when one sees what end was being aimed at, even if unsuccessfully, in and by the process. In this respect, this sort of causality is quite distinct

from the efficient causality with which most experimental
sciences are concerned, which requires reference only to a
general law and a prior state. For the prior state, in purposive
causality, must contain an ineliminable reference to some
future (purposed) state, in order to be explanatory. The
physical description of a cat's movements over a short stretch
of time does not have the explanatory force of the insight
that the cat is stalking a mouse. But, to say the latter, one has
to interpret the feline movements in terms of a future,
desired goal.

It is extremely difficult to decide whether there are irreducibly purposive causes in nature. This is both because it
is often unclear whether certain processes are purposive or
not, and because it is just possible that most, or even all, such
explanations may be reduced to general covering-law explanations in some sophisticated way. There are five main
candidates for purposive explanation: human and animal
action, the phenomena of organic life, the order of physical
laws, the beauty of nature and the general process of evolution. In each case, it is quite reasonable to ask whether a full
explanation of the process would require a reference to purposive causality. The answer is most obviously 'yes', in the
case of human action. There are those who argue that the
activities of human agents can in principle be accounted for
in terms of non-purposive laws, those of physics, for instance.
I do not think any such account has been properly made out,
and a good assessment of such arguments is given by Richard
Taylor, in *Action and Purpose* (1966).

In any case, one may still hold that purposive explanation
is necessary to a full explanation, in that any explanation
which did not mention purposes and values would omit completely many important data of thought and intention which
are certainly part of the phenomena, but with which physics
does not deal. Conceptually, an account in terms of the production of one event out of a preceding one in accordance
with a general law of the form 'Whenever x then y' is quite

different from an account of the production of an event as directed towards the realization of a future state. One may try to put the latter into the form of efficient causality by saying, 'Whenever p has the intention to bring about x, and all other conditions are right, x will be brought about'. The trouble is that this proposition is untestable, in a way that truly empirical propositions are not. I can state the laws of physics precisely and generally; I can specify the initial conditions exactly; then I can predict the outcome with certainty (within the limits of indeterminacy, in sub-atomic physics). But what general laws connecting intentions with resultant states are there, except the vacuous one that an intention to do x will, other things being equal, result in the occurrence of x? The connection between an intention and its actualization is partly analytic; I can only describe the intention by mentioning the state which is its goal, so there can be no general laws connecting independently specified intentions and their consequences. Furthermore, I cannot specify intentions precisely; they may be confused, unconscious or not communicated. My only real test of whether an intention exists is to observe a piece of behaviour to see if it is intentional, to see if it appears to be directed to a goal. But that uses the very form of purposive causality I am seeking to eliminate. Finally, I cannot predict the outcome of intentions with certainty. It is just not true that the presence of an intention infallibly brings about its intended result, in some way exactly predictable. My intention to be rich will, of course, give a general guide to the sorts of actions I am likely to do, but it will very rarely give rise to any exact predictions about what I do on particular occasions. I may turn down the offer of a large sum of money because, despite my intention to be rich, I also do not want to take bribes. But what prior way is there of measuring competing intentions, beliefs and values, so as to predict what they will cause on all occasions?

The only hope for the attempted assimilation of purposive causality to efficient causality is to trace some one-to-one correlation of specific intentions with physical states of the brain; and then to claim that the brain-states do give rise to predictable outcomes in accordance with general laws of neurophysiology. The empirically testable part of this claim is that, given knowledge of a certain state of the brain, one can predict each subsequent state thereafter. I accept that this may be testable, in principle (though it may not, because of the impossibility of isolating actual brains from all physical influences which may affect the predictions); if it was shown to be true, it would, as far as I can see, decisively refute human freedom, purposive causality and God, as I conceive him. Clearly, then, I think it will not be shown to be true, and the mere possibility that it could be true is no threat to its actual falsity. But there is a non-empirical part of the claim, too, namely, that intentions can be correlated with brain-states. I can see no way of doing that systematically, since we depend solely on the agent's reports, at least for the sophisticated intentions which humans have. And each personal intention is so complex and specific that one could never have enough precise data to set up the desired correlation. I conclude that the programme of eliminating purposive causality completely by reducing it to efficient causality is part of a wider metaphysical commitment to materialism, which entails the rejection of theism. As such, it must be assessed on its merits as a consistent, comprehensive conceptual interpretation of reality. Certain empirical discoveries are relevant to such assessment, but it is unlikely, and perhaps impossible, that one will get any decisive test, as one would for most scientific hypotheses.

Oddly enough, the reasons which make materialism attractive are very similar to those which make theism attractive: the desire for intellectual simplicity and elegance, belief in the universality of general laws and insistence upon one general ontology, or theory of what exists. But I think that materialism misconceives the nature of simplicity. It seeks a sort of highest common factor view, explaining the complex appearances of the world in terms of those elements which are common to every part of it. But then one has to eliminate all the other, uncommon, unique or anomalous factors by reducing them in some way to the simple. So consciousness, purpose, value, beauty and morality become by-products or even illusions of the physical structure of the central nervous system. Materialism is the victory of the abstract over the concrete, of the simple over the complex, of brute fact over intelligible necessity. If simplicity is an intellectual virtue, it is not the process of ruthlessly suppressing the complex and denying its existence. It must be combined with adequacy, with richness of explanatory force, so that it places the riotous complexity of things within an overall scheme whose structure may be simple but whose content may be infinitely complex. This will not be done be denying consciousness, purpose and value, but by uniting them coherently within one intelligible framework.

A recent attempt to use the criterion of simplicity on behalf of theism is to be found in Richard Swinburne's *The Existence of God* (1979). He argues that theism is more likely than any rival supposition because it has high prior probability and great explanatory power. By the latter, he means that a God would be likely to make a world like this, so he makes the world probable; and that the world on its own is very unlikely, since it is so complex, finite and particular. By the former, he basically means that God is the simplest possible hypothesis which could explain the world. He is one being, whose powers, being unlimited, are the simplest possible, and who explains absolutely everything. So no theory could explain more things better, or be simpler. Naturally, I am very sympathetic to this argument, but there are three connected points where I have reservations. They are: the very wide use of the idea of simplicity; the assertion that this form of argument to God is one of inductive probability; and the claim that God is the ultimate brute fact, not a logically necessary being.

I have defended the view that God is a logically necessary being. If I am right, the chief reason Swinburne gives for denying that there can be deductive arguments for God — namely, that 'the non-existence of God is logically compatible with the existence of the universe' (p. 120) — disappears. Nevertheless, deductive arguments from the world to God are impossible, because such arguments can only explicate what is already in their premisses. He maintains that the only alternative is some form of inductive argument, asserting what is likely to exist. An induction proceeds from the singular to the general or from the known to the unknown on the basis of perceived analogies. In the case of theism, one first makes an analogy between the world as a whole and some part of the world, for instance, a watch or a machine. Then one argues, that since machines have makers, so the world must have a maker, to explain its machine-like nature. In Swinburne's version of this argument, the analogy is between the order and law-likeness of physical laws and the sorts of order produced by humans. The existence of a few simple kinds of fundamental particles with a uniformity of powers, he says, leads one to compare nature as a whole with human artefacts. This similarity increases the probability that the world is ordered by an intelligent being — even though it does not make it probable, taken on its own.

This is precisely the sort of inductive argument so devastatingly considered by David Hume, in the *Dialogues Concerning Natural Religion.* Hume objects that the universe is very different from any particular effect within it, that it is an unreliable induction which argues from a small part to a huge whole and that induction is inappropriate in assessing the nature of the universe anyway, since the universe is by definition unique and all-embracing. 'Does not the great disproportion bar all inference?' he asks. How can one establish an inductive probability which applies to one unique reality, and which can never be independently checked? I am inclined to think that Hume is right; the main difficulty of starting an inductive argument to God lies in establishing that there is a sufficiently close analogy between the universe and some events within it for an induction to work. The well-known argument from analogy to the existence of other minds has the advantage that other bodies are very like mine in many ways; its disadvantage is that I only have one case of a testable correlation between private mental events and bodily events to go on (my own). This is insufficient to give rise to a reliable generalization. The argument from analogy to the existence of a cosmic mind may be said to have the advantage that there are many cases of observed correlations between order and mental causality — all human artefacts. But the whole problem lies in establishing that the 'order of nature' is like a human artefact. Is the universe as a whole like a house, or a watch, or even like a computer? I think it is fairly clear that there is no objective decision-procedure. If it was probable that God exists, why do all observers not agree? The analogy is at best ambiguous. So that, whereas in the other minds case, everyone really knows that there are other minds, and the problem is only to try to say what really justifies that belief; in the cosmic mind case, many people sincerely deny its existence, finding the similarity-gap too great.

How does one decide whether the universe is relevantly similar to an artefact? I do not think, as a matter of fact, that one tries. That seems to me a philosopher's misconstruction of what is involved, a misconstruction arising from the dogma that all reasoning must be either deductive or inductive. What one does is to postulate the axiom of intelligibility, and ask what form of explanation best fits observed reality. One model is that of deductive rationalism, by which there is a sufficient reason for everything, and that is the one that posits a necessary, immutable uncaused cause. But that model eliminates contingency, freedom and the choice of value, so that a model of creative choice of value comes in to supplement it. On this model, a process is explained if it is seen as aimed at realizing something of intrinsic value. This

model alone does not explain how those values come to be as
they are, or how it is that there can exist a being capable of
aiming at value. So it needs the first model to show the necessity of its basic postulate. All this is at the level of what constitutes a complete explanation of the world. The models are
not derived by induction from particular sense-experiences;
there is no way in which the facts alone can generate the
theories in the light of which they are interpreted. The interpretations are brought to the facts, as conjectures or postulates.

Yet they are not merely arbitrary, as though anything
might have done. They are conjectures as to what would
satisfy a wholly rational being; not because of any subjective
constitution it may have, but because of the very structure of
reason itself. A complete explanation does not satisfy just
because a certain sort of being happens not to feel the need
to ask any further, like a child being satisfied by some fairly
arbitrary explanation of things. It satisfies because there is,
objectively, no need remaining on the side of reason. And,
though we cannot actually give that explanation, we can see
what sort of thing it would be, and some of its implications.

It is when we bring such a conjecture to the facts that we
see what may be called the probability of its applying; by this
is meant, not any quantifiable measure of probability, but a
necessarily subjective judgement as to how well it seems to
apply, or how well we can fit the facts, without distortion,
into the theory. In metaphysical conjectures, there is no
empirical falsification, no deductive testing, as Popper terms
it, of a direct sort. Instead, we appeal to such rational criteria
as consistency, coherence, adequacy, simplicity, comprehensiveness and integrating power. There is no good inductive
argument to the existence of an explanation for order in
nature. But, if we conjecture that there is an explanation, we
may ask how well it enables the facts to be integrated and
understood.

This is just what Swinburne does, in practice. For he

assumes the principle that 'the simple is more likely to exist than the complex' (p. 106). I see no reason whatever to suppose that is true, in the absence of some prior presupposition. How is one supposed to know what is likely to exist, without waiting to see? As Hume argued, anything is as likely as anything else, inductively, until we see what actually happens. So this principle of simplicity is an a priori principle, a conjecture. Moreover, I do not think 'simplicity' is in fact quite what Swinburne has in mind. For is it really simpler to suppose that a cosmic 'person' (as Swinburne terms God) brings the world into being than that there are one or two ultimate physical laws and an initial state such as is posited by the big bang theory, from which all things develop by random motion? It is noteworthy that Swinburne appeals precisely to the existence of a few simple kinds of basic particles as a fact requiring further explanation, in his version of the design argument. Thus he seems to think that simplicity requires explanation. For what can account for such simplicity, when it seems very improbable? But he cannot have it both ways; either simplicity is probable, in which case appeal to God only complicates the story further, bringing in intentions, infinite powers, omniscience and so forth; or simplicity is improbable, and there is no inductive route to God.

Swinburne holds that God is the simplest kind of being, because he is one, he provides the most general sort of explanation and his powers, being unlimited, are the simplest possible. It does not seem to me very plausible to say that the necessary and incomprehensibly great creator of all is a very simple being (the technical sense of 'simplicity' used by Aquinas is not the one in question here). Nor is it clear to me that it would not be simpler to eliminate him from the scene altogether. Nor can I see how the possession of an unlimited, infinite degree of power is simpler than the possession of some finite degree of it. True, I can always ask, 'Why this degree, and no other?' But, since I have to end up with a brute fact anyway, it is simpler to end with some precise degree of power than with the wholly mysterious notion of an infinite degree (that is, no precise degree at all).

All these troubles are connected, for it is not simplicity that is required. It is necessity and comprehensiveness and absoluteness of explanation. God does not explain better because he is simpler. Simplicity needs explanation, too. What one requires is the postulate of a being *a se*, existing from itself alone. Such a being is one, because there can logically only be one being *a se*. Its powers are unlimited, because there is no other being to limit them. Its existence is not probable (a peculiar sort of probability, that has no set of comparable cases against which to measure itself) but necessary. Simplicity comes in, when, on rational grounds, we prefer a simpler to a more complicated explanation of the same phenomena, where there is otherwise little or nothing to choose. Thus, for instance, one might prefer the hypothesis of one god to two, if there is no sign of conflict in the universe. But the test can hardly be applied when what is in question is whether the universe can be explained theistically at all. For that is the question, whether there is an absolute explanation for the universe; and whether part of this explanation must be in terms of purposive causality. There is no way of proceeding inductively to answer this question; the universe is too unique and all-embracing an object to give a reliable analogy. So what we do is make a postulate. And I suggest that the appropriate postulate is not 'The simple is more likely', but 'The self-explanatory is necessary'. With that postulate, one can return to the observed nature of the universe, to try to judge whether it shows the sorts of order, intelligible causality, value and purpose which should follow from one's postulate. There is no deduction of God from some facts about the universe, and there is no induction from particular experiences. The existence of God is probable, only in the sense that it may seem more or less likely to us that there is an absolute and purposive explanation. In itself, it is necessary; and the measure of subjective probability is not a theory-neutral perception of close similarity between human artefacts and the universe as a whole, but a synoptic judgement about the extent to which the perceived universe confirms the basic postulate of theism.

God is, as I have argued, either necessary or impossible; so the argument is one of coherence, not of collecting evidence. Data are relevant to helping to fill out a coherent concept; they help to suggest its content, and, naturally, they must not contradict it. So we say, 'This seems to be coherent' or 'This does not seem to fit'; in neither case are we using the canons of inductive inference. Swinburne is only able to set up an inductive model by putting all the weight into the assertion that the simple is probable. But that is not inductively established; and, once it is assumed, one no longer needs induction, but rather, assessments of simplicity. Similarly, we do not argue that, because human artefacts are produced by minds, therefore the ordered universe is probably mind-produced. Rather, we have a puzzle about explaining the universe, with the sorts of order it contains, and, in looking for an explanatory model, we postulate either deductive necessity or creative purpose, or some combination of both. The 'purpose' model is plainly suggested by reflection on human purposive activity, but it does not generate an inductive probability any more than we infer that, because the universe is like a piece of mathematics, it probably obeys the principle of sufficient reason. We have to apply the model first of all, before we can interpret the facts in the light of it; the alleged similarity does not exist to be perceived until we establish it by rational speculation. We do not see an obviously purposive universe, from which we can then infer a designing mind. All the argument has to go to show that the universe can reasonably be interpreted as purposive. And that is a matter of showing an explanatory postulate to be plausible, not a matter of arguing from known to unknown by clear analogy.

It is certainly plausible to hold that there are some instan-

ces of final causality in nature, namely, in human beings. But
are there others? One natural move is to ascribe it to everything, as Aristotle and Aquinas did. Aquinas's 'Fifth Way' for
demonstrating the existence of God was based on the premiss
that 'an orderedness of actions to an end is observed in all
bodies obeying natural laws' (*Summa Theologiae,* qu. 2, art. 3).
If this is saying that all events have final causes, it seems implausible and unfruitful. Not all events seem to culminate in
desirable end-states, and the search for purposes does not
lead to illuminating generalizations about nature, as the
search for efficient causes does. But what Aquinas seems to
have in mind is simply the orderedness of physical law itself,
the fact that objects do not move entirely at random, but do
obey general laws. Moreover, these laws are, as Leibniz put it,
coordinated so as to obtain 'as much variety as possible, but
with the greatest order possible' (*Monadology,* 58). Does not
the very order, harmony and universality of physical law
argue for an organizing intelligence?

As Hume himself (or at least Philo) concedes in the *Dialogues* (pt. 11), 'the perfect uniformity and agreement of the
parts of the universe' show a unity of cause, and count
against the postulate of many competing or diverse gods. It
appears to be true that everything in the universe is guided
by natural law, by principles of mathematical elegance and
order which are astonishing in their complexity and harmony. One may well now argue that laws, being abstract
principles in accordance with which objects are to act, but
not being themselves objects, have just that character of
'prior ideas, being realized in the future' which requires the
postulate of an ordering mind. Certainly, the view sometimes
expressed, that physical laws are only descriptions of how
objects act, seems very implausible. The physical sciences
predict with certainty events which happen light years from
earth, and do not countenance the possibility that objects
may just happen to agree with their predictions. In happily
legislating for the whole universe, they assume the prescrip-

tive rule of law in the universe. They thus assume that there is, in objective reality, a basis for such a prescription of order. However remote the analogy from limited human minds, there is here a commitment to a causality by idea or concept, the determination of the concrete by abstract principle. Reality, it may be said, is not a collection of internally un-related data; it is a whole whose parts change intelligibly in accordance with general laws, and which are brought to be by concepts as well as by preceding physical data.

Suppose this to be so, however, it may not follow that one is licensed in inferring to a God beyond the world. There may be, suggests Philo, in part 6 of the *Dialogues*, 'an eternal in-herent principle of order to the world', which requires no external being to explain it. And Flew puts the point in his own way by espousing what he calls the 'Stratonician prin-ciple': namely, that 'all qualities observed in things are quali-ties belonging by natural right to those things themselves' (*God and Philosophy*, p. 69). This is a rejection of the picture of a random collection of unordered particles, which need to be organized by some exterior force. Why should the order not be inherent in nature itself? Why not, indeed? But then, as Philo again says in part 4, 'By supposing it to contain the principle of its order within itself, we really assert it to be God'. Precisely. Even if order is considered as a principle inherent in the world, it differs from disorder, chance or accident by incorporating a principle of concrete change in accordance with abstract principle, of causality through con-ception. If one wishes to call final causality an inherent character of the universe, very well; one is thereby saying that the universe contains a conceptual basis of ordered change, that the world is mind-like in its most basic constitu-tion. Such pantheism is after all a form of theism; what re-mains to be asked is whether there may not be other reasons for considering this mental aspect of reality to be self-subsis-tent in a way that the world is not.

It is thus not implausible to take the orderedness of the

world under physical laws as a sign of a purposive constitution of nature. But appeal to such order does not assign a valued state for the sake of which the process exists. Can one further discern particular purposes in nature, which can be taken as ends of its existence? The most obvious place to look is at the phenomena of sentient existence. It may seem to be just unwarranted anthropomorphism to suppose that the whole universe exists in order to produce beings like us. 'What peculiar privilege has this little agitation of the brain which we call thought?', asks Philo in part 2. But in fact the case is deeper than a simple partiality for our own species. For if there is to be value at all, it is plausible to argue that there must exist some consciousness which values it. It is not the mere existence of beauty which is valuable, but its appreciation by some consciousness. So the concept of value is connected with that of sentience. In view of this, it is not irrational to see sentience itself as a possible goal, a condition of the existence of any value. If one is looking for valuable states which the universe may be conceived to exist in order to realize, they may well lie in certain states of consciousness.

One may go further than this. For we may suppose, with Aquinas, that 'the goodness of a thing consists in its being desirable' (*Summa Theologiae,* qu. 5, art. 1). So that a state has value if it is one that a fully rational being, in full knowledge of the consequences, would desire. There may be an infinite number of different things which such beings desire, but, if one desires anything at all, then one also desires to be conscious of doing or having it. One may not desire bare consciousness for itself alone; one may not desire it at all, when allied with extreme pain, for example. But one desires consciousness as a condition of anything else one desires. Thus awareness is desirable if anything else is; in that sense it is an intrinsic value, or a condition of any such value.

One not only desires to be aware; one desires that awareness to be pleasurable. There is no one common quality of pleasure, nor is the best state necessarily the one that gives most pleasure, on some measurable scale. Pleasure is not one thing that all desire, but all desire what pleases them. Pleasure is desired for its own sake, in that one needs no further reason for choosing something other than that it gives one pleasure. Pleasure may therefore be added to simple awareness, as an intrinsic value and a condition of anything else one values.

Now one may say that pleasure results from the contemplation of what is known; to know deeply is preferable to neglecting or passing over briefly, or knowing in a merely abstract sense. The most desirable form of awareness is a full and deep appreciation, a delighting in what is known; and this involves an intense activity of the knowing mind, which is itself pleasurable. One may object that it cannot be desirable to delight in what is evil. That is true; but even so, it is better to know evil for what it is, to see it in all its consequences and inner nature. So even then, the sort of awareness one values most highly is that which apprehends most fully by a sensitive and active apprehension. An intense, sensitive and appreciative consciousness is the highest degree of a state of intrinsic value, and is thus well fitted to be the final purpose of an ordered sequence of events.

If that is so, then any being capable of such consciousness has good reason to avoid anything which does, or could, threaten to impede or destroy it. And it has good reason to espouse anything which can preserve or extend its capacity for sensitive awareness. Any such being would therefore have good reason for desiring power rather than weakness; for to be weak is to be at the mercy of things other than separate oneself, but to be powerful is to be capable of preserving desired states, whatever they are. Similarly, it would have good reason to desire wisdom rather than foolishness; for to be wise is to know the most effective ways to achieve what one desires. And it will desire freedom rather than compulsion; for to be free is to be able to choose what one wants, rather than merely what one is compelled to have.

Just as knowledge is not mere accumulation of facts, but fully sensitive appreciation, so freedom is not just indeterminateness of will, but is a positive impulse to creative effort, which brings delight in its own exercise. Just as appreciation is an intrinsic value, being valued for its own sake and as a condition of all other values, so creativity is an intrinsic value, as the power of producing many possible valued states, wisely and without compulsion, and as an intense degree of a property which one always has a good reason to choose, if one chooses any value whatsoever, the property of being self-determining.

The argument has been that, if one is to discern purposes in nature, they must consist in valuable states which the processes of nature may be seen as directed to bringing about. There may be an indefinitely large number of valuable states; but it is a condition of anything being valued at all, that there must exist awareness and pleasure or happiness. And, if there is reason for valuing anything, there is always good reason for valuing knowledge, power, wisdom and free creativity, for they preserve or extend one's capacity for attaining or retaining whatever one values. It is therefore not just anthropomorphic partiality which makes us believe that a consciousness not wholly unlike ours could be the final cause of the universe. In any possible world, it is better to be conscious, happy, powerful, knowing, wise and free than not. For without reference to the self-determining choice of a sentient being, the very notion of 'better or worse', of value itself, fails of application. The good is what a free being would reasonably choose, given its feelings and knowledge of possibilities. So if one is to talk of value at all, one is committed to a substantive set of values, which are intrinsic in the sense defined, that any rational being would have good reason to desire them, if it desires anything at all.

It accordingly turns out that, if the universe was purposively constituted, one might expect to find it resulting in the existence of a maximally self-determining, creative, sensitive and beatific being. Whatever other values such a being possessed, it would realize maximal value only if it possessed at least these. Even if a maximally valuable being is not to be realized, these properties will represent intrinsic values in any possible world. So their existence will tend to confirm the hypothesis that the world is purposive.

We have been considering the choices of a rational being as if it existed in complete isolation, and asking what it would have good reason to choose, as if no other choosing agents need be considered. But suppose, as is vastly more probable in any universe containing many developing elements, that there are many rational agents of the same general sort. Are there any general values which will govern the relationships of these agents to each other? It seems clear that there are, even though the situation will become very complex in particular cases, as they relate in various ways to one another. Since it is an intrinsic value for each agent to be happy, powerful, knowing, wise and free, every one has good reason to espouse anything which preserves or enhances these properties, and to avoid anything which diminishes or destroys them. Thus the maximally valuable state will be one in which each agent finds happiness by increasing the happiness of others, increases its own power by co-operation with others, increases its knowledge by appreciating sympathetically the experiences of others, enhances its wisdom by devising the best way of correlating the desires of all and increases its freedom by combining with others to provide projects and purposes which could not be attained alone. Any state in which one agent increases its powers at the cost of diminishing the powers of others will be less valuable than one in which a similar increase can be gained for all. It may be that such an ideal maximization can rarely be found in practice, but it remains an ideal. It is a state of mutual co-operation and involvement which every agent has good reason to desire, if and in so far as it is possible. This is to say that, if one desires anything as an intrinsic value (a value for any rational agent), one is committed to accepting it as a value for all rational agents. So one is committed to accepting the co-operative pursuit of freely chosen purposes as a value for any set of roughly similar rational agents. All this is not to say what one will or should do in particular social situations, where one usually has to trade off benefits for some against disadvantages for others, or deal with seemingly irreconcilable conflicts of interest. It is, however, to say that any reflective rational agent is committed to accepting social co-operation as a fundamental value; other things being equal, there is good reason for choosing it rather than conflict. So one might expect to find a purposive universe resulting in the existence of a community of rational agents, helping, sharing and co-operating with one another's freely chosen purposes; or at least in a community which had the possibility of developing towards such an ideal. If the argument sketched here is acceptable, that will be true in any possible universe; it is established simply from a consideration of what value is, not from observation of this actual universe.

Having established what a purposive universe would be like, one now needs to ask whether this universe is sufficiently like that. It is certainly the case that beings which are sentient and self-determining have resulted from the operation of apparently general physical principles, developing from inorganic states of mass, velocity and position by various mechanisms which gradually and continuously produce emergent properties. It does not seem at all strained to see the process of evolution as a development aimed at the production of intelligent life, even though one cannot refute the view that the process is one of complete chance, however purposive it looks. And it is entirely natural to take the phenomena of organic life as oriented to an end. Organisms appear to be systems so ordered that their parts function to maintain the whole, and the whole is ordered so as to become an apt vehicle for sentience.

In all this, one is not looking to find some purpose imposed from outside on a passive and inert nature. One is discovering in the structure and being of matter itself a nisus or tendency towards the development of sentient life. But that is just what one would expect of an inherently purposive process. As such, it must be conceived as directed to an end which is conceptually envisaged at the beginning of the process, and, in that sense, as the product of an ordering mind.

The fact that the universe appears to agree with what one would antecedently expect of a purposive process does not prove that it is purposive. One cannot disprove the possibility that it may all be a product of chance, just as it is theoretically possible that three monkeys typing at random would one day write the Bible. But one can say that the universe looks consistent with the activity of a purposing mind. So one may suggest, as John Hick does in *Faith and Knowledge,* that God is a 'seeing-as' postulate; one sees the world as purposive, with the aid of the concept of God, as purposing mind.

I think this notion of 'seeing-as' is a valuable and illuminating one, but, to my mind, Professor Hick moves a little too quickly when he holds that what we see is the world as encounter with a personal will, a dynamic sovereign Lord. My suggestion is that we may see the world as purposive, as exemplifying what one may call an archetypal causality, an inner direction towards the realization of certain values which are present, as archetypes, in the basis of nature itself. We may see it thus without allegiance to a form of intuitive personalism. The form of immanent conceptual causality I am supposing does not license or rely on the sort of personalist model favoured by Hick. I think religious experience is too essentially vague and diverse to lead directly to the sort of 'perceptual belief' in a 'sheerly given personal reality' of which he speaks (*Arguments for the Existence of God,* p. 112). He seems to admit as much on page 119, where he rather speaks of many 'aspects of one immensely complex and rich divine reality'; such an admission must qualify any claim to direct apprehension of a holy will, and suggest that God is rather more like an explanatory hypothesis than a perceptual belief, after all.

Seeing the divine reality as a personal will is just one form of religious experience. However intense experience may be, it must be articulated and modified by the general conceptual interpretation within which it occurs. Both explanatory interpretation and spiritual experience are necessary; it is the latter aspect which, for example, Wisdom's influential paper, 'Gods' neglects, when it deals with the question of whether the world is mind-like from a seemingly wholly speculative standpoint. But the two cannot be divorced, and I believe that reflection on religious experience, in the context of our more general reasonings about the nature of the world, will lead to a more complex and less directly personalist understanding of God than Hick suggests. For the moment, it will be sufficient for me to stress that by 'seeing-as' I do not mean a quasi-perception or intuition, but a general way of apprehending and reacting to the experienced world, namely, as expressive of purposes and values.

The design argument, at least in this form, is not an inference; we are not moving by induction from one small part of the universe to a very dissimilar part, to the whole universe or to a unique case. Just as we do not infer to the existence of other minds, but interpret the movements of certain bodies as interactions and responses with us, so we do not need to *infer* to the existence of God, but we can interpret events in the universe as *expressive of* intention and value. We need to interpret the data of experience with the aid of concepts, if we are to have knowledge at all. And the concept of God is one of these concepts which we apply to experienced data in order to see the world as purposive.

Admittedly, the concept is not necessary to having any knowledge at all. We can refuse to see the world as purposive, and no vast harm will be done to experimental science as yet.

The claim must be that the notion of God is needed for a completely adequate account of the world. Hume's dictum that we should only ascribe to a cause what is absolutely and minimally necessary for explaining its effect is countered by another dictum, that we should seek an ultimate explanatory scheme for the world which will be the simplest, most coherent, adequate, elegant, consistent and fruitful. The drive for unity, coherence and intelligibility is as deep a human drive as the drive to economy; and the principle of economy must rightly take its place as only one intellectual desideratum within a coherent overall conceptual picture. What the design argument evokes, then, is not a deductive conclusion from irrefutable premisses, showing that a God must be the explanation of purpose in the universe. Rather, it evokes a vision of a purposive and intelligible universe, united by one being in whom value, freedom and meaning coincide. God is not the minimum postulate accounting for design; he is the ultimate focus of all human rational acts, the integrating concept of a total interpretative scheme for reality. Such a concept clarifies as different strands of human experience point towards it, as the completion of their own proper endeavour.

Philosophers can hold strangely impoverished ideas of rationality. One of the most limiting of all is the idea that all reasoning is either inductive or deductive. Inductive reasoning consists in observing a number of examples of a certain sort of thing, and then in generalizing to make assertions that things similar in some respects will also be similar in others. It is, of course, very important to be able to generalize from particular cases, and to calculate probabilities from observed samples, but it is a rather low-grade rational activity. Deductive reasoning, which consists in eliciting the implications of sets of premisses, can also rise to great heights of sophistication in mathematics; but without such things as imaginative flair and intuitive insight, it could be performed as well or better by fairly simple computers.

When one speaks of a person being rational in ordinary

life, one does not primarily have either of these skills in mind — though someone lacking them would hardly qualify as rational. What one has in mind are such things as these: that one can select all the relevant facts to a certain enquiry; that one can rank them in order of importance; that one can judge tendencies or discern patterns among a jumble of disparate data; that one's decisions are such that they issue in desired goals. Rationality is a sort of skill in which people vary enormously; and the precise nature of the skill varies according to the area it is exercised in.

Suppose one asks, for example, whether a certain philosophical view is reasonable, whether it has been rationally arrived at. One will look at the deductive links of the arguments, but one will be much more interested in the philosopher's vision of reality, his understanding of the nature of the world. An irrational view will be one which conflicts with much evidence, or which begins from arbitrary premisses, or which has no connection with ordinary beliefs, desires or hopes. But one is primarily looking for the introduction of a new key idea which puts things in a different perspective, a re-orientating idea for organizing our intellectual framework. The highest use of philosophical reason lies in the conceiving and application of a new organizing idea, or a new interpretation of an existing idea, which enables one to build up a new, more comprehensive scheme for understanding the world. That is a function of imaginative and creative reason. It is certainly not deductive, for that only works out what is already there. And it is not inductive either. It is a presuppositional activity, which picks out and organizes the primary data in a particular imaginative way; it is like constructing a pattern for the world to fit into, from the creative extension of a number of clues. These clues are discerned by creative reason, contemplating the world synoptically and evaluating its most significant features and fitting them into an overall pattern.

Examples of the use of creative reason are the Greek

hypothesis that the cosmos was a rational order, expressing general intelligible principles; the Galilean hypothesis that the order of nature was constructed on mathematical principles, as a set of mathematically expressible general laws; and the Leibnizian theory that the world is a spiritual reality, perceived in an obscure or confused way by the human senses. Naturally, creative reason does not always arrive at true theories; its guiding ideas may be too partial or idiosyncratic. Nor does it always work at that level of generality. The use of imaginative insight and re-orientation within the application of a particular scientific theory is essential to the progress of the physical sciences. The working physicist who puzzles about how to overcome the problem of tarnishing in silver does not work by methodical induction; he tries various ideas, explores many analogous techniques, but is always guided by the search for new, more comprehensive patterns of explanation which may suggest an answer to his particular problem. And that is a matter of judgement, synoptic vision and patterning skill, as well as of sheer luck.

So, when one speaks of God, induction is a wholly inappropriate methodology. God is not an object like others, to be inferred from various occurrences in the world. Nor is deduction any use, since one cannot get out of a deductive argument what one does not first put in. The truth is that the idea of God is an organizing idea, the most general one possible, which enables one's view of the world to be patterned in a particular way. Since there is not just one idea of God, there will be various patterns available to theists, which will overlap at various points in complex ways. To speak of the rationality of that idea is to speak of the imaginative richness of its conception, the synoptic range of vision it makes possible, the integration it achieves among diverse aspects of human life and thought.

What I am suggesting is that to see nature as designed is not to see it as a relatively self-contained machine, from which one can infer a designer by induction. It is, rather, to see it as expressing an immanent archetypal causality, the temporal unfolding of a set of intelligible forms. This is, in a way, a return to Aristotelian rather than Newtonian categories, and that may be considered a retrograde step. The designer comes in, not as a separate person constructing the machine, but as the place of forms, the immaterial reality in which they exist. Mind becomes the inner constitution of reality, not a separate, external entity; purpose lies in the immanent direction of temporal processes to the realization of values, things of which it is true that it is good to exist. It may be said that the progress of modern science has been due, above all else, to the elimination of purpose from the material universe, to positing the inflexible rule of universal law. That is probably true. Aristotelian physics, with its theory of the four elements and of rationally intuitable essences, was incapable of producing the quantitative measurements which have been essential to the development of the mechanistic sciences. Yet number is not inimical to a purposive view of nature. On the contrary, mathematical order, as Pythagoras saw, is a primary expression of purposive structure; though, naturally, a study of the order itself will not disclose the purposes it subserves. The notion of purpose is essentially connected with the idea of value, and it is because science eschews talk of values that it can ignore purpose.

The time may be close, however, when that is no longer so. The isolation and exploration of the quantitative basis of natural order leaves man free to impose his own purposes on the world, to elaborate a technology subservient to his own purposes. And we have now reached a stage at which technology is able to modify human life and consciousness itself. Can we, dare we, rest content with an approach to the world which gives us the techniques to modify it at will, while giving us no clues as to how it should be modified, except the dangerous facts of our own desires? The recent proliferation of ecological sciences may suggest a renewed appreciation of

the values which exist in nature, and which need to be con-
served and respected. And it may be that unless we can re-
store a view of nature as oriented towards values which are
implicit in its own structure, we shall find that in a universe
from which all values have been obliterated, technology
becomes an amoral monster which completely destroys its
human progenitors.

The idea of God, as an interpretative or regulative model in
terms of which to see the universe, can preserve the value and
significance of human life and endeavour, and it will govern
our understanding in many different areas. Revelation may
be seen in sequences of events which make clear particular or
ultimate purposes; the purpose of God in creation will be the
realization of objective archetypes conceived in the divine
mind; moral values will be seen as ideals which define the
true natures, the final ends of all natural objects. Overall, one
may see the whole of one's experience as an interaction with
a personal being whose nature is revealed in his creation: 'For
the invisible things of him from the creation of the world are
clearly seen, being understood by the things that are made'
(Rom. 1: 20). Of course, it must be remembered that the
notion of God as a person is only a model; he is not like a
human person, and indeed, one may better conceive him
more impersonally, as the conceptual causality immanent in
all reality, rather than as some sort of external interferer.
Nevertheless, it will become appropriate to adopt the general
attitudes of worship (of seeking and celebrating objective
value), gratitude (for the blessings which have been intentionally caused, and are not just accidental or fortuitous),
dependence (upon a reality which is ordered to the realization of good), trust (that the good will triumph) and practical
love in pursuing goals which are rooted in the nature of
reality, and are not merely subjective preferences. The life of
worship and prayer will be, not just a subservient relation to
various spiritual powers; but a seeking for union with the
mind which orders all things, and an attempt to align oneself

with its purposes. Thus the religious life will take on coherence and unity, and be integrally related to the rest of
experience.

If one adopts the theistic postulate, one will also be able to
see the many beauties of the world, from the splendour of
the stars to the crystalline structure of atoms, from the bril-
liant colouring of flowers to the subtle patterns of birdsong,
as achievements of form and pattern which reveal, and are
intended to reveal, the character of their ultimate cause as
creative mind. If one sees beauty, not as a subjective response
to neutral data, but as an objective value which functions as a
final cause, shaping matter to its manifold realizations and
transformations, this naturally suggests and coheres with the
idea of a cosmic mind, as the objective 'place of Forms', the
reality in which those values, as archetypes, exist, and which
seeks to realize them in the world in new and creative ways.
Then the contemplation of nature becomes the dim apprehension of the manifested forms and patterns of the Divine
mind and its values, which are realized and apprehended fully
by that mind itself.

Once more, the pattern of argument is not an inductive
one, from human works of art to nature as the handicraft of
a Divine artist. It is the proposal of a distinctive way of seeing
or interpreting nature; namely, as purposively ordered to express objectively beautiful forms. If one is inclined to see
beauty as objectively in things, to be discovered and apprehended by men, not invented or imputed by them, then it is
quite implausible to take it as a property which simply happens to result from certain combinations of particles. For it is
a value whose realizations depend upon a complex arrange-
ment of parts, and is thus most naturally seen as the final end
of such arrangements. Again, conceptual causality, shaping
matter by means of archetypes of value, is the natural interpretative model which enables one to see nature as ordered to
the expression of objective beauty.

Once archetypal causality has been postulated, it extends

its regulative function over biology, history and morality too. The amazing variety of organic life forms can be seen as realizations of archetypes, ordering the parts to the maintenance of total organic systems, and urging the species on to further experimental realizations of them. The interrelated systems of ecology and biology may be seen as exhibiting the same sort of experimental creativity as is found in works of art, the same joy in sheer inventiveness and even the same wastefulness of materials and abandonment of certain projects. This is not a world in which a loving heavenly parent forever prevents his children from suffering harm. It is a world in which archetypes of system, unity-in-diversity and value express themselves in a wild creative urge for manifestation. The cosmic mind is, it seems, no great respecter of individuals, biologically speaking; but it strives incessantly to produce system, harmony and the existence of the largest number of compossible values. Whether the experimental sciences of biology need to take such archetypal causality into account is not yet clear. It is possible that they can ignore it, as irrelevant to their predictive and manipulative concerns. On the other hand, it may yet turn out that holistic explanation — explaining the parts in terms of the whole within which they have a place and function — has an essential part to play in the biology of the future. Either way, the fact that a certain view is true does not imply that it has any role to play in quantifiable scientific investigation.

The interpretation of history and morality, too, is modified by the postulate of an immanent cosmic mind. Where the world is purposively ordered, one may expect to find intimations of those purposes at various points of history, and morality will largely consist in the discovery and pursuit of such purposes. Nature and morality will not be disconnected, or even at odds, as they are in some views of the world. Since there are objective moral goals in nature, one may reasonably hope for a fulfilment of one's moral strivings, and one may hope to find a rational morality in the fulfilment of the true or archetypal natures of material things. So it can be seen that the regulative model of God has implications for the way in which various different areas of human experience are interpreted, and it relates those areas in a coherent and intelligible way. A consideration of each of these areas in isolation may suggest the theistic postulate. Its real force can only be seen when its integrating function between the areas of morality, history, biology, religion and art, and its capacity for evoking a unified vision of the universe which gives personal life and its values an enduring significance is recognized. One can by no means prove that such a postulate is necessary; what justifies it is its provision of a total imaginative interpretation of reality, which also provides the basis for a distinctive practical commitment to the pursuit of objective demands and values, and to the practice of worship and prayer.

I conclude that it is reasonable to see signs of purpose and design in nature, and that these can best be conceived in terms of the model of an immanent conceptual causality, a unitary mind-like ground which shapes the world towards the realization of intrinsically valuable states. But does this really get one beyond the notion of a world designer to the idea of a perfect creator?

The world-architect may be limited, as the Demiurge of whom Plato speaks in the *Timaeus,* is, both by the nature of the materials he works with and by his own limited abilities. The Demiurge has to work with pre-existing matter, and he must use as a model for his design the intelligible world of Forms, which is independently and necessarily what it is: 'Intelligence controlled necessity by persuading it for the most part to bring about the best result (*Timaeus,* 48). The Forms themselves, the patterns of all things, and the material stuff in which they are embodied, remain outside Divine control; there is no explanation forthcoming of how the architect comes to have the being and nature he has, how it happens that matter is malleable to his purposes, at least to some extent, and what the relation is between the world-architect and the Forms which are the basis of his purposes. All these problems were propounded but left completely unresolved by Plato; they were his bequest to both the Christian and pagan philosophers who wished to unite popular belief in the gods with a rational theism, and articulate that theism in a way more satisfactory to the demands of the intellect.

Aristotle simplified the scheme slightly by eliminating an independent world of Forms. But his god, too, has to co-exist with an everlastingly existent matter. He does not take any active part in shaping the world at all, for he is changelessly immersed in the contemplation of his own eternal perfection. The world is moved by its own desire to reflect his perfections in itself: 'the final cause moves by being loved' (*Metaphysics*, Λ7, 1072b). It was left to Augustine to propound a coherent idea of a Divine Spirit, which could both contain all Forms as ideas, necessarily constituting its essential nature, and act to shape the world in accordance with them.

The design argument, as I have construed it, suggests the idea of such a ground of conceptual causality, realizing values in the world. One must think of this ground as having immense power, for it shapes the whole universe in accordance with general laws, and realizes its purposes over vast stretches of space and time. It must have knowledge of all the archetypal values, some of which it chooses to bring into being, and of all it has actually caused to be, in order to be able to go on shaping it in desired ways. If every event is to fit into one unitary system, aimed at some set of valuable ends, the Demiurge must have immense knowledge of the facts. It must be immensely good; for benevolence consists in bringing values into being, and the whole purpose of the Demiurge is to realize a great set of values. It must be immensely wise, to set up such a very complex system of simple laws and rich consequences. And it will be natural to think that it is supremely happy, finding pleasure in the exercise of its own power, in contemplation of the values it produces, and perhaps even in sharing in the good of the creatures it forms.

Thus the Demiurge may have limited powers, and may have to work with pre-existing matter, and its own existence and nature may be inexplicable; but it must at least be a being of immense intrinsic value, exemplifying to a very great degree those values which have been characterized as intrinsic in any possible world. There may be something which has greater power than the Demiurge, which can make better or bigger worlds, with greater values in them. But, as far as this universe is concerned, no being in it could have greater power than the Demiurge. For, on the theory, it shapes the laws which lay down the powers of all beings coming to exist in accordance with them. Whatever powers beings in this universe have, they depend upon the formative power of the Demiurge. It is perhaps conceivable that the Demiurge could make a being more powerful than itself, able to make a world more wisely, or knowing more or able to destroy the Demiurge. But if so, it would be something which no longer had to depend on the Demiurge for its form and nature. Having been designed, it was thereafter self-sufficient. Such a being would no longer be part of this universe, dependent upon its laws for all the powers it possessed. Frankenstein can make a monster more powerful than its maker, but only because the doctor is unable to control the physical laws which enable them both to exist at all. If Frankenstein had learned mastery of the laws of nature themselves, he could at any time destroy any being whose existence depended upon them. So no being which depends for its existence on the laws of nature which the Demiurge controls, can have greater overall power than its maker. Conversely, any being which passes beyond the control of the Demiurge no longer depends on the laws of this universe for its being. We may say, then, that the Demiurge is necessarily more powerful than any finite being within the universe which it controls; it is almighty, in having power over all creatures within the universe which it forms.

The idea that matter is not a reality independent of God, but is dependent wholly upon God for its existence, is not strictly entailed by the design argument. But it is strongly suggested by it. Just as the unity of physical laws suggests one world-architect, so the universality and necessity of those laws suggests the dependence of matter upon the Divine law-giver. An architect is limited by the nature of his material, and must shape it in ways it permits. But the laws of physics are not just patterns into which some pre-existent material can be placed, like architect's plans for a house. The laws of physics state the dispositional properties of matter itself, which are constitutive of its very existence as matter. If one takes away all known physical laws from matter, there is nothing left. Matter is constituted by law, in a way that architect's plans are not. So, if the order, universality, necessity and intelligibility of law suggests a designer, it also suggests rather more than that: namely, a being who not only shapes matter, but constitutes it as the sort of thing it is.

That is to say that, before the law-governing activity of God, there is no matter at all. There is certainly no sign of some kind of medium which resists the scope or necessity of physical law. Since the whole universe seems to be entirely and perfectly governed by law, the hypothesis of an independent matter becomes otiose. It is simpler to say that matter itself, in its internal constitution, depends for its existence upon God. God will be not just the architect of the world, but its creator. This is a vast gain in intelligibility; one no longer has a mysteriously uncreated matter to cope with, in addition to God. There is just one ultimate reality, from which all other things derive.

Thus the doctrine of creation is a very suitable postulate for explaining the actual nature of this universe. In the course of the discussion, we have been able to discover something about the sorts of states that would be of intrinsic value in any possible universe. They have been specified as the personal perfections of knowledge, power, wisdom, happiness and (where there is a plurality of sentient beings) co-operation, or mutual benevolence. Orthodox theists hold that God is perfect, a being of maximal possible value, so it seems that he must at least possess these personal perfections maximally. I have suggested that the creator will possess these perfections to a very great degree, but it has not been shown that the creator does possess them maximally. As the indefegatible Hume puts it, 'This world, for all he knows, is very faulty and imperfect, compared to a superior standard, and was only the first rude essay of some infant deity, who afterwards abandoned it, ashamed of his lame performance' (*Dialogues*, pt. 5). Can this universe really sustain the postulate of a perfect creator? And can a coherent idea of a maximal possessor of these personal perfections be formed? These are the issues that must next concern us, before going on to see how the notions of the perfect creator and of the necessary self-existent being can be satisfactorily combined.

6 　 The Divine Attributes

The argument from purposiveness in the universe, taken alone, cannot establish that there exists a creator who possesses intrinsic values maximally, though it can lend strong support to such an idea. It must be remembered, however, that the argument does not proceed on its own, as if one must first argue to the existence of an architect, then to a creator and finally to a perfect creator. On the contrary, all theistic arguments are explorations of the fundamental idea of a self-explanatory and therefore self-existent being. It is only when, because of an acceptance of freedom and contingency in the universe, this being is conceived as bringing the world to be by free choice, by creation, that the question of purpose and value really arises. It is then that one needs to test the adequacy of one's conjecture of a self-existent creator by asking whether signs of purpose can be found in the world. And, in the process, one is able to specify certain personal perfections of the creator by discovering the nature of the values that are intrinsic in every possible world.

When the idea of a world-architect is seen to be the specification of the notion of a self-existent being, it is at once apparent that it will possess intrinsic values in a logically maximal way. Such a being will be necessary and immutable; thus it will exist in every possible world, with just the nature that it has. It will be the underived cause of all beings other than itself, since it is the one and only self-existent, and must explain the existence of all other derivative beings. Whatever powers any beings have, in any possible world, they will be derived from the self-existent, and cannot logically exist independently of it. So the self-existent cannot create a being more powerful than itself. For the greatest possible power, with respect to any particular thing, is the power to make or destroy it; and the greatest possible power in general is the power to make or destroy everything. But the existence of every being in all possible worlds derives at every time from the self-existent; there is no escape from its power and thus it possesses maximal power. From that attribute, as I shall argue, maximal possession of the other personal perfections follows. However, it may still be doubted whether the idea of maximal possession of such attributes is coherent.

The idea of omnipotence, for instance, is admittedly a difficult one to formulate. It is not satisfactory to say that God can do absolutely anything — make it rain when it is dry and sunny, make the laws of logic false or make colourless objects blue. Accordingly, many theists have adopted Aquinas's view that an omnipotent being is one which can do anything which is logically possible. The laws of logic are restrictions on the Divine being, but not avoidable ones; they are absolutely necessary. However, it has been pointed out that there are logically possible things God cannot do: he cannot do evil or destroy himself or climb a mountain or make a stone he cannot lift. The obvious thing to say, in reply, is that, though such things can be stated in the form of consistent propositions, they are incompatible with states which already exist, including the nature of God himself. God is good, indestructible, immaterial and has power over all material things. These properties of God are immutable; so no being can do anything which implies that God does not possess them. Now I have held that, in a broad sense of logical necessity, it is logically necessary that such a being, God, exists. So it is logically impossible that there could exist any state which implied the non-existence of such a God. Therefore no being, not even God, can do anything that contradicts the nature of God. God cannot do evil or make stones he is unable to lift; the former is incompatible with his wisdom and goodness, and the latter would entail renouncing his omnipotence, and is incompatible with the immutable possession of the Divine powers. If one defines God as a being of illimitable power, then nothing at all, not even his own acts, can limit that power. Even an infinitely powerful being can only do what is logically possible; so God cannot make anything that would limit the possession of his power — and this includes stones too heavy for him to lift, or beings beyond his power to control.

There is a sense in which God can limit his own power, for instance, by creating free beings which have the power of autonomous decision, which God is unable to control as long as that freedom remains. But this is simply a limitation on the exercise of power, not on its possession. God always and necessarily possesses the power to control beings totally. But he may choose not to exercise that power, for the sake of some other end which he wills, like the existence of moral freedom in creatures. It is only in that sense that God may be said to be self-limiting.

The whole notion of limits on the Divine being is often subject to logical confusion; for it may be held that if God is infinite, then he can be limited in no way at all, since any limit makes God finite, or excludes some property from him. For example, if one says that God is omnipotent, one thereby excludes the property which is the negation of omnipotence, namely, lack of power. If one says that he is wise, one excludes foolishness from his being. If one calls him perfect, one excludes imperfection, and so on. In a sense, therefore, the possession of any such properties makes God finite, in excluding something from his being. But clearly, if one did not do that, one could say nothing at all of God. Belief in a God to whom no nameable properties may be ascribed is indistinguishable from atheism. So one needs to distinguish between the sorts of limits which are necessarily ascribable to God, if he is to be named at all, and the sorts of limits which are removable restrictions on his perfection. One may say that God is logically limited by necessarily possessing those properties which are involved in the notion of a perfect, self-existent being. But he is unlimited, in that nothing other than his own nature or decision limits him, that the number and sort of values he can actualize is infinite, and that the intrinsic values of his being are maximally possessed. God is limited in necessarily having the nature he has; but this is a condition, not a restriction, of his perfection. He is unlimited in that he can do anything compatible with his own nature.

But one may suspect that this is a mere tautology. If one says that an omnipotent being is any being which can do any logically possible thing, compatibly with its nature, then one might have cases such as the following, constructed by Plantinga: 'The man who is capable only of scratching his ear scratches his ear' (*God and Other Minds*, p. 168). Thus he does every action which it is logically possible for him, given his nature, to do; and it may seem that, though he can only do one thing, he is omnipotent, by the definition. The difference is, however, that the power which the ear-scratcher possesses is a logically contingent power; that is, his nature is both contingent and finite, and, of course, derivative from God's power. As I have argued, the only being the nature of which can be necessary is the one and only self-existent being. It is not because it must be compatible with the nature of the agent (whatever that is) that Divine power is limited in certain ways, but because it must be compatible with all logically necessary truths — which include truths about the nature of God, though not about the nature of anything else. Accordingly, if it is accepted that it is logically necessary that God exists, one can accept Aquinas's definition of omnipotence: that an omnipotent being is a being which possesses the power to do anything logically possible.

It thus appears that the difficulties with the definition of omnipotence which have beset many philosophers follow from the refusal to say that God exists by logical necessity. But if one thinks that the state represented by any proposition whatsoever is logically possible, then one cannot define omnipotence as the power to perform any logically possible action. For no being can both create everything other than itself and also make something not made by God; yet these two acts are logically possible, in that neither is overtly self-contradictory. If the agent does the first act, it is God; if it does the second, it is not; so it cannot do both. It follows that no being can do all logically possible acts.

Kenny suggests that one might amend the definition by talking not of actual performances of acts, but of powers to act. An omnipotent being might then be one that has every power which it is logically possible to possess (*The God of the Philosophers*, p. 96), though it may not always be able to exercise every power, because of other powers it has exercised. But, as he recognizes, this does not help; for no being can both have the power to create all things other than itself, and the power to create something God does not create. In the former case, it is still God; yet even God does not have the power to sin or die or change his nature. There are some powers that only God can have and some that God cannot have; so we are stuck.

So Kenny is forced to deny the applicability of a general definition of 'omnipotence' to God, and say that the omnipotence of God is the power to do anything that is logically possible for an immutable, good, spiritual being. This, of course, cannot be a general definition of omnipotence; it is rather a specification of the greatest power that God could have. Nevertheless, if God is defined as the creator, with the power to make or destroy anything other than himself, then one might say that the power of God is greater than the power of anything else. So God would possess the greatest possible power any being could possess, while not strictly possessing the power to do anything that is logically possible, in general. Divine power is unlimited by any other being; for there is no other being uncreated by God. It is complete power of making and destroying all finite things (all things that depend on him for existence); thus it is power over all possible things. And it is power to bring about any state which is compatible with his immutable nature.

The greatest possible power is the power of a being which is the only underived cause of everything other than itself. It is power unlimited and unsurpassable by any other being. There is no reason, perhaps, why unsurpassable power should be the power to do every logically possible thing. But if there is a creator, it will possess unsurpassable power, simply by possessing the power to make or destroy all possible things.

It is not quite enough to say that God's power is unsurpassable, in the sense that it is always actually greater than anything else. For that could mean that, while there could be no greater power, there could be many powers independent of God. Whereas a greater degree of power would be power over everything — unlimited or infinite power, such that no being other than God possesses any power except powers given by God. Again, it is not just that no being can have any power over God; for any immutable being (like a number) is such that no other being can bring it into existence or destroy it; yet it is not thereby omnipotent. What is being asserted is that all possible powers must derive from God. Thus one could define an omnipotent being as a being such that all powers other than its own necessarily derive from it, and cannot limit or surpass its power.

This definition clearly entails that any omnipotent being must be a creator, but it does not give any clue as to what limits of power there may be within the creator himself. It is not said that he can do anything logically possible; or even, as Kenny suggests, that he can do everything logically possible for such a being as he is. But it is asserted that no being is omnipotent if any independent powers exist, or any powers limiting or surpassing his (except in the sense that he may refrain from exercising some power if he wishes, though the capacity itself cannot be limited). It may be held that this is the greatest possible power, and that it is senseless to ask whether there could be more powerful possible creators. If God is the ultimate brute fact, he may be omnipotent in this sense, and to ask about further logical possibilities is idle, since one just has to accept what is ultimately the case.

I am not satisfied with this answer, though I think it is the best that can be done, if the logical necessity of God is denied. The trouble is that one is looking, not just for the greatest actual power, but for the greatest possible power. One is inescapably cast into the realm of logical possibility; and one wants to say that the being of greatest possible power must be one which could not logically possess greater power. Its power is not just unsurpassable as a matter of fact, given this universe as it happens to be. It must be logically unsurpassable — unsurpassable in every possible world. As Kenny puts it, it must possess 'all logically possible powers which it is logically possible for a being with the attributes of God to possess' (*The God of the Philosophers,* p. 98). This requires that God is not just the creator of this universe — so that there could be other creators of other universes — but that he is, necessarily, the creator of any possible thing other than himself. But if one accepts that such a notion of logical unsurpassability is a coherent one — and it seems clearly so to me — one is committed to the idea of the logical necessity of Divine existence. For if it is necessarily true, in all possible worlds, that x is creator of everything other than itself, then it is necessarily true that x exists in all possible worlds, that it necessarily exists. The only exception is the possible world in which nothing at all exists. But — apart from the argument already given for doubting the coherence of this suggestion — it is enough to say that, if anything at all exists, then God exists. What must exist if anything exists is an admirable candidate for logical necessity.

Thus I have proposed two possible definitions of omnipotence. One, assuming the coherence of necessary existence, states, in a traditional way, that an omnipotent being is one that can do anything logically possible (compatible with existing logical necessities, including the existence of an underived source of all other powers). That is the one I favour. The other works with a notion of factual, brute omnipotence, and states that an omnipotent being is one which has unlimited and unsurpassed power (indeed, unsurpassable power, in the factual sense that, given the nature of the world, as dependent wholly on God as first cause, nothing in the world can have more power to make or destroy than God). I think this is what Geach has in mind when he prefers to speak of God as almighty, rather than as omnipotent (*Providence and Evil*), as having power over all things. Unlimited and unsurpassable power would certainly be maximal power, where the idea of necessary existence is thought to be incoherent; and such maximal power would be possessed by a creator of this universe. The advantage that I believe the former definition to possess is that it coheres better with the axiom of intelligibility, which is the foundation of rational theology; and it enables one to assert that there could not possibly be a more powerful being in a different possible (or even actual) universe. How can one say that God has total power over all possible things, unless one sees him as the foundation of all possibility, the one without whom nothing would be possible, and thus as the one without whom no world could possibly exist?

The Platonic Demiurge, which might fairly be called almighty, possesses immense (but not total) power over everything it forms (but not over every possible existent). The design argument provides good reason for thinking that an even greater being, a maximally powerful being, exists. For it gives some reason for supposing that the material world itself is brought into being by a god, by free choice of a unique set of values. God, as creator, will possess total power over every possible thing (for there can be nothing he does not create). This corroborates the conclusion of the intelligibility-arguments, that all things derive from one self-explanatory being *a se,* not only the creator of this universe, but the creator of any possible universe. Hume's supposition, that this world is 'the first rude essay of some infant deity', errs in postulating that there can be many gods, and that they can learn and develop by trial and error. There is only one being *a se,* which is what it is in every possible world, and which is immutable in its general nature. The design argument is not an introductory first step towards this conclusion. It is, rather, the specification of the causal activity of the being *a se* as a free, purposive causality, as creation rather than emanation.

There is, then, a coherent idea of a maximally powerful being: a being of unlimited and unsurpassable power, capable of doing everything logically possible, in the broader sense. The arguments from the intelligibility of the world, in concluding to the existence of a being *a se,* necessarily conclude to the existence of such an omnipotent being. The design argument further specifies the form of this maximal power as dynamic capacity, exercised in the pursuit of freely chosen ends. God has unlimited potency for realizing the ends he chooses; he possesses maximal intrinsic value in at least this respect.

This idea of maximal power entails the existence of knowledge in the Divine Being, and, indeed, of maximal knowledge, of omniscience. One might be tempted to think of God as an unconscious source of all beings, producing creatures by blind necessity. But such power would be very far from unsurpassable. There can be immense forces which are unconscious — the wind, electricity, the sea. But that sort of undirected, blind power is precisely not a power to do anything; it is well-defined and limited by necessity. The wind cannot help blowing as it does, for it does not know what it is doing. It would be a much greater degree of power which was able to act or not to act, which was able to choose what to do; and that requires knowledge of what it is possible to do. One might even say that it is contradictory to ascribe omnipotence to a being which has not got the power to know everything. If it is possible to be omniscient, then the omnipotent being must be able to be omniscient; and, since it is better to know what one is doing than not, it must actually be omniscient. And if the universe originates from God by an act of free choice, one must conceive God as knowing the things he could create and as having some criterion of rational choice. He must be conceived as knowing all possible worlds and things, and being able to choose for a good reason between them. So he must be conceived as omniscient, free and rational.

The definition of omniscience shares the problems of the definition of omnipotence, and they can be resolved in much the same way. It is not enough, as Kenny suggests (*The God of the Philosophers*, p. 10), to define omniscience in the formula: 'For all p, if p, then X knows that p'. It is precisely because he is satisfied with that definition that he later concludes that 'there cannot ... be a timeless, immutable, omniscient, omnipotent, all-good being' (p. 121). The main problem is that of future contingents, of God's knowledge of events which lie in our future. On the simple formula here cited, which is a timeless proposition, God must know truths at every time, and any tensed truth at every time. As Kenny rightly says, it is difficult to see how one can both hold this and exonerate God from responsibility for the future sins of his creatures. If God knows eternally what I will do in the future, then it seems that my acts must be fully determined in advance; so that I cannot be free, in the sense that, at the moment of action, I can act otherwise than I do. I intend to deal with this problem in detail later. It is sufficient to note at this point that if there are things which do not yet exist in any sense, which have not yet even been conceived as actualized possibles — that is, if temporality is real, even in God — then it is not required of a maximally knowing being that he knows them; for no possible being can know *as actual* what is not yet actual. It is a coherent supposition that, where p is an event future in time relative to t, and where its actualization

depends to some extent upon the free choice of some creature at t, no being before t could know that p will be true. For
some p, if p, then x will not know that p, under certain conditions (namely, at and before t). This is true even of a maximally knowing being, though, naturally, such a being will
know p as actual, as soon as its actualization is effected; and
it may know that p will be actual, as soon as its actualization
has been determined for certain. An omniscient being, if it is
temporal, can know for certain whatever in the future it
determines, to the extent that it determines it, but not absolutely everything. If this is a limitation on omniscience, it
is logically unavoidable, for any temporal being (and the
temporality of the perfect being will be defended in the next
chapter). Incidentally, this account coheres perfectly well
with biblical accounts of prophecy; for they rarely, if ever,
prophecy exactly what is to happen. On the contrary, they
are often provisional and very inexact in detail, and they
need to be sensitively interpreted to make them into prophecies at all. (Note the transference of prophecies about
David's successor as king, in 1 Sam. 7, for instance, to a far
Messianic future. Jews and Christians still disagree about
whether that prophecy has been fulfilled, and, if so, how).

So the admission of freedom to creatures places a certain
sort of restriction on omniscience. But there is a host of
other restrictions. If God knows everything, does he have my
sense-perceptions? Does he feel my pleasure and pain? Or
have my appreciation of beauty? Can he know my knowledge
and my ignorance, my sin and repentance, as I do? For if not,
there are many things God cannot know; he cannot know
anything in the way that creatures do. Kenny and Geach
apparently have few reservations about assenting to this.
Kenny puts some emphasis on the point that one can know
p without knowing it in the same way as someone else. So
God can know that I am in pain, without knowing it by
acquaintance, as I do. But this is still an enormous restriction
on omniscience. 'Knowing that' someone is in pain is very far

removed from knowing what it is like for them to be in pain, from sympathizing with them. To rule out knowledge by acquaintance from omniscience is to rule out the most important and personal items of knowledge completely. This is in line with the traditional ascription of impassability to God; since he cannot be affected by creatures in any way, he cannot feel pleasure or pain because of their actions or feelings. Geach goes so far as to say that it is an instance of the pathetic fallacy to ascribe sympathy to God, for God has no feelings. I am not at all convinced that it would be a symptom of perfection to lack all feeling. God, of course, has no senses and no nervous system; whatever feelings he might have are unlikely to be very similar to human feelings. But are we to say that he does not appreciate the beauty of creation at all? That he takes no pleasure in well-doing and feels no sorrow at sin?

It seems to me an extraordinarily attentuated notion of knowledge which views it as the accurate tabulation of true propositions, registered passionlessly, as if on some cosmic computer. The whole idea that omniscience could consist in simply knowing more true propositions than any other being strikes me as grotesque. Is one who really knows us not one who feels our sorrow and grieves with us? Rejoices in our happiness and knows the unformulable secrets of our hearts? There are infinite gradations and subtleties in our emotional lives, which cannot be put into any set of propositions; human feelings, in all their complexity, exist. But what set of true propositions fully and accurately captures their nature? The whole idea of there being one accurate, complete set of propositions which expresses the whole truth about my personal being is a misconception.

In this case, Kenny's formula for omniscience fails because it is too narrow. There is an indefinitely large number of things which can be known (known by acquaintance) which cannot be adequately put into the form of propositional truths. What set of propositions would exhaustively specify what I know by looking out of the window now? Even if some set did — and I do not think it does for a moment — all one would have would be sets of general, relatively abstract terms, dependent upon our vocabulary and cognitive limitations, which would necessarily omit the particularity and unique concreteness of the experience. Is that all we are prepared to credit God with?

In any case, we are conceiving God as choosing to actualize a world in virtue of the sort of values it instantiates. But how are we to conceive of God as knowing that x is a value? It is true that we can just put it into the form of a proposition, and say that God knows that 'x is a value' is true. But, as I suggested in talking of intrinsic values, it does not make sense to speak of something as a value, without reference to pleasure and choice. x is a value if it is worthy of choice; but, for a being of purely intellectual, dispassionate knowledge, why should anything be worthy of choice? One might construe such propositions as 'x is beautiful' as saying that 'x produces a certain sort of appreciative pleasure in p', where p is some human person. Then, when God knows that x is beautiful, he really knows that p believes x to be beautiful. Similarly, when he knows that a sensation is painful, he really knows that p feels pain from that sensation. But can God really know that something is beautiful or painful without feeling appreciation or pain? Even in the tradition, God is spoken of as possessing beatitude, which surely involves some sort of pleasure, even if only in his own perfections. A being who felt no pleasure would lack the intrinsic value of happiness; and so could not be a perfect being. But, if God feels pleasure, that feeling is not just extrinsically connected to his knowledge; as though knowledge had nothing to do with what gave pleasure. Pleasure is found precisely in knowing something; there is even a distinctive sort of pleasure in purely intellectual knowledge. Divine omniscience is not the acquiring of the most information; it is the most sensitive and complete acquaintance with values (and disvalues also), which alone provides a basis for the rational choice of good and avoidance of evil. In other words, it must be the greatest possible form of knowledge by acquaintance. So any account of it in terms of purely intellectual knowledge of propositions is radically defective.

When one says that omniscience is knowledge of everything it is logically possible to know, one may thus exclude future occurrences which have not yet been decided; and one must include knowledge by acquaintance, which propositional knowledge cannot fully cover, and which is the basis of rational evaluation and is therefore not wholly dispassionate. As with omnipotence, one may say that Divine knowledge is illimitable − there is nothing in things which obstructs or impedes it. It is also unsurpassable − no possible being could have greater knowledge. But, since we cannot hope to understand the Divine nature fully, we need not expect to have any very clear idea of what it is like to be omniscient. All we need to possess is good reason to think the notion coherent, and to think that some being possesses it. This we have, if we conceive of the omnipotent creator as choosing to create this universe for the sake of its particular goodness.

One may therefore say that, given certain plausible assumptions, the Divine properties of omnipotence and omniscience are mutually entailing. All omnipotent causes of explicable contingent beings are omniscient; otherwise, they would not be able freely to cause any or all really possible things. A 'blind omnipotence' could produce only entirely necessary or random things; it could not act for reasons, which involves knowledge of what one can choose. So, if the world is contingent, omnipotence entails omniscience. Similarly, if omniscience is necessarily possessed, then the omniscient being must know that nothing could possibly exist that it does not know. And for it to know that with certainty, it would have to know that no being was capable of producing something it did not know; that is, that no possible being could transcend its knowledge. That could only be guaranteed if the omniscient being was itself more powerful than any other possible being, if it was omnipotent. So, while it is possible that one could have a powerless or weak being which happened to know everything, an all-knowing weakling, no being which is necessarily omniscient, as the self-existent creator must be, can fail to be omnipotent.

Now if God is omnipotent and omniscient, one may equally plausibly argue that he will be perfectly good. Knowing all possible things, and being able to choose any of them, he will reasonably choose the best. Or so it would seem. But this assumes both that goodness is a property of things (some things are good in themselves) and that there is a best com-possible actualization of states. If one rejects the latter view, as I have already done, one can still say that God will always choose what is good, because of its goodness. And, though he cannot choose a logically best set of states for himself — since there is no such thing — he can choose an actually best set of states, better than any others which he causes to exist. That may seem rather a selfish thing to do; but it must be remembered that goodness is not divisible, so that giving more of it to one being involves taking some away from another being. The reason God can possess more good than any other being is simply that he is necessarily more powerful and knowledge-able, so that he is capable of unlimited creativity and appre-ciation; all created beings can only possess finite amounts of those goods, and all others which depend upon them. God can certainly will the existence of a vast number of goods to other beings; but their good can never, in the nature of the case, equal his own.

If one asks what sort of goods God will possess, it is vir-tually impossible to say. The list Anselm gives, in defining the 'greatest conceivable being', is as follows: life, wisdom, power, truth, justice, beatitude, being, reason, beauty, in-corruptibility, unity, immutability and eternity (*Monologion*, 15, 16). This is no doubt not intended to be a complete list; these are examples of properties which it is better for an un-

created, immaterial being to possess than not. It is noteworthy, however, that they fall neatly into the two lists of
perfections, metaphysical and personal, which have emerged
from the cosmological and teleological arguments, respectively. Eternity entails immutability and incorruptibility; with
unity, it is one of the five metaphysical perfections which
underlie the rational intelligibility of the universe (the others
being aseity or self-existence, necessity and exhaustive determination of all possibility or logical completeness). Life,
being and truth are preconditons of the possession of any
perfections. And wisdom and reason, power, justice (as
impartial love), beatitude and beauty (as appreciative knowledge) are the five personal perfections which maximize the
conditions of rational choice, and so underlie the structure of
being as directed to the realization of valuable goals.

Anselm, like all Platonists, takes the abstract essence to be
more real than the particular; so he sees God as 'beauty'
rather than as an individual who delights in the contemplation of beauty. He also sees God as self-sufficient; so what
God contemplates must be part of himself; so he is the
beautiful as well as its contemplator. We might say that in
contemplating the beautiful forms inherent in his uncreated
nature, God is supremely happy. It seems that, in seeking an
idea of perfection, one seeks for the highest degree of personal perfections (those that a rational being would find
worthy of choice). One then seeks to eliminate from this idea
all possible defects which could arise from dependence on
other realities. Thus one achieves the idea of a self-existent
rational agent. The self-existence guards against the changes
and mischances of fortune. The rationality is what gives the
self-existent whatever positive value it has.

So the metaphysical perfections may be called formal;
they say that, whatever God is, he is independent in existence, but do not give any more positive knowledge of what
he is. Similarly, the personal perfections do not specify the
objects of Divine knowledge, creativity, happiness and love.

They could be his own ideas, but once the Platonic principle is overthrown, it is no longer realistic to say, even of God's ideas, that they are more real than individuals (as Anselm could); so that God would be the same, with or without a world. The fact is that, as far as we can see, all beautiful, lovable and shapeable objects are in the created universe. We cannot imagine a beautiful object that has no shape or form in space or time; an object of love which is not distinct from the lover (only thus avoiding inescapable narcissism); an expression of free creativity that has no independent being to be used and moulded.

God may, of course, be self-complete and thus wholly unimaginable, as many early Christian fathers agreed. Thus Gregory of Nyssa wrote, 'Knowledge of the divine nature is inaccessible . . . to every created intelligence' (*The Life of Moses,* II, 163). And Basil said, 'Knowledge of the divine essence consists in the perception of his incomprehensibility' (Letter 234). We cannot conceive that part of his being which is the object of his knowledge. But, while allowing that to be true, it may be that our only ways of ascribing perfection to God compel us to conceive him as related to beings other than himself, a world that, though created, may have its own proper autonomy and plurality. So we could ascribe to God the basic intrinsic personal values, those involved in any rational choice of purposes. We can ascribe to him all properties implied in his self-existence. Beyond that, though we may agree that he could possess an infinite number of properties inconceivable to us, we must admit that we can only think of positive goods as belonging to this finite universe, as objects of his knowledge, creativity and love. If we are asked to think of God without any universe, we simply cannot do it. The Aristotelian *noesis noeseos,* contemplating himself in one endless intellectual act, only really makes sense when Platonism lives on. For then, in knowing himself, God will know every possible thing in a way more real even than if it was actual. But if, in the modern manner, one takes ideas to be abstract possibilities, the picture of a god totally absorbed in his own daydreams is not a very attractive one. The Aristotelian god is the cosmic solipsist, and it is hardly surprising that, when roughly baptized into Christianity, he tends to become the self-absorbed tyrant, never really granting value or autonomy to creatures.

This does not mean that God cannot exist without any world. But it does mean we cannot envisage the mode of his existence; it is completely beyond thought or conception. All we can say is that, since we think of God as self-existent, yet related to the world in action, knowing and love, it may, for all we know, be possible for him to exist unrelated to any world. But what is the importance of saying that? It can only be to plead the ultimate agnosticism of all human thought about ultimate reality, the superiority of God to the limits of human thought.

God on his own cannot be self-giving love; for there is nothing to give himself to. To say that he gives one part of himself to another part of himself splits him into parts in an unacceptable way. Nor can one think of a solitary God as freely creative; for again, without any creation, he obviously cannot make anything. We cannot do other than conceive him as possessing a sort of self-sufficient logical completeness and totally unimaginable sort of perfection; as knowing and delighting in this being completely, as the 'sat-cit-ananda' (being-consciousness-bliss) of Indian theology. The accusation of egoism really is irrelevant to such a conception. For it is not that God has regard to his own self-interest as opposed to that of others — there are no others. And it is not that he remains introverted when he should be extroverted and loving. Although many sorts of creation would be good, and each would introduce a different sort of additional good to the sum of reality, it cannot be said that it is morally necessary to bring them about. Can one seriously argue that it would be better for God to create some world than not? It has already been remarked that, since there is no best possible world, there is no particular world which God should bring about. He may bring about any good world; but must he bring about some good world? I think not, for the following reason. Since there is no best possible world, it must be admitted that God could always have brought about a better world than he did. So it cannot be the case, in general, that he must always bring about the greatest good. Now the existence of God is itself a very great good. Thus it is not obligatory for God to create anything other than himself. The existence of some created world would certainly add to the sum of goods in existence; but it would also change the sorts of good which exist in God. Perhaps one might say that the cost of finite creation is to introduce suffering and opposition into the being of God. God must be thought as containing in himself the possibility of such a change. But, given that God cannot increase the sum of goods without changing the kinds of goods there are, it does not seem to be true that God must increase the sum of goods. We may ask, 'Was it better that God died on a cross for men, than that he remained in supreme beatitude without creation?' Though we may acknowledge that it is good that he did, since it is a condition of our existence, we cannot say that it is unequivocally better, or that, even if it were, it was better in such a way that God would be morally compelled to bring it about. In short, the position of a God deciding whether or not to create anything other than himself is quite different from the position of someone wondering whether to give himself to others in love, when there are some others.

The mistake the Scholastics made was to suppose that, since God could have been totally self-sufficient, he always is so, even when he has actually created a universe. The Divine power to bring about beings other than himself could have remained unrealized; the Divine love, the sharing of Divine life with others, could have remained one of the many unrealized and non-compossible properties of God. Of such a God, one can say almost nothing, though one can point to it as an ultimate beyond which places limits on human speculation, and prompts a certain caution in theological speech. However, God has created. So, when we speak of God, we do so in terms which relate him to this creation; we speak of him as creator, not as self-sufficient being.

Thus, when we select the personal perfections of God as those which are involved in any rational choice of purposes, we are naturally and inevitably considering God as creator, as the one who has chosen such purposes in creation. It is hardly surprising, then, that the attribution of these properties in their fullest sense of creativity, sharing and loving, to God seems to entail the existence of creation, of some objects of the Divine making, loving and knowing. So it does; and, if God really has these properties, then he is no longer the completely self-sufficient eternal one; he is one who both expresses and creatively determines his own nature in relation to creatures. However, one could still properly speak of a God who had not created as omnipotent, omniscient, happy, wise and good, even though these properties were derived by a consideration of the intrinsic values involved in rational choice. For one must say, of such a God, that he has the power to create any world, even if he creates none; he has the capacity to know all created things, and actually knows his own being perfectly; he would act wisely and well in any world; and he is good, in containing the greatest actual amount of value, as well as the archetypes of all possible values. So, while one cannot imagine God without a world, one can, and indeed must, ascribe to him many capacities which are realized in creating this, or any, world. He must also be ascribed actual power, consciousness and value in particular forms wholly beyond our imagining. The form which these properties take in our world, however, is such as to call for a modification of the Aristotelian notion of God as an unchangeably self-sufficient, impassible being. Divine creativity is a co-operation with creatures in achieving many freely chosen goals. Divine knowledge is a sharing in the awarenesses of creatures, which modifies the quality of Divine beatitude. Divine benevolence is a continual outflowing from the Divine being, to provide many sorts of perfection and happiness for others.

Such co-operative and sharing love is one of the greatest values, as it is only in transcending self and relating to others that one truly becomes a person, a developing, self-expressive being discovering itself in the forms of its social relationships. Thus God can become a person, in this sense, only as he creates some community of rational agents in relation to which his own perfection can be expressed. In creation, God determines his own being as interactive; in doing so, he actualizes his own nature as the one who is love, in particular, contingent ways.

That is not to say that God does not know what he is until he confronts other objects; and, interacting with them, discovers for the first time his own potential. God, as basis of all possibles, knows perfectly all he is, and cannot discover anything new about himself, which previously existed unknown and unconsidered. Yet suppose that God determines himself as a consciousness which must be orientated to objects. Then it will be true that he can only realize what he is in relating to such objects. As Hegel puts it, 'Spirit becomes for itself or actual . . . in the form of the other' (*Philosophy of Religion*, vol. 1, B.2). For God, of course, there can be no absolutely other; there can be only what he posits. But in that positing, he sets free forces of autonomy which provide him with opportunities for creative fashioning, appreciative contemplation and responsive activity. Nor is this a cosmic exercise in filling out the consciousness of God, as though finite beings were mere adjuncts to his self-realization. Once others are created, they are in themselves — even though in a dependent and relative and conditioned way — real centres of value and awareness. Objects are never merely objects, screens for consciousness to project its empty intentionality upon. They, too, have interiority, or, at least, they intrinsically possess the potential for interiority, for the inner awareness which preserves its inviolable individuality, even in face of the all-encompassing creator. Thus when God returns to himself from his encounter with the other, he returns enriched, as now including a community of imperishable wills, not a seamless undifferentiated unity, but a richly diverse and internally related, complex unity, which is the endless manifestation of the destiny of God, the self-existent creator and reconciler of all things.

Thus God, may bring to be a world of real objects, of individual, autonomous, partially self-directing beings, in order that he may determine his own being in a particular way by giving it to what is beyond himself. Those objects cannot be of no concern to the God who creates them. Love is the culmination of objectivity; its intense desire to unite and unify presupposes a separateness, which is yet not utterly alien and independent, but never at root capable of existence entirely apart and alone. All beings become objects to themselves, exist for themselves, by first being objectified, externalized and so projected into the truly other; from whence they must return reshaped and transfigured. If God creates in the free exercise of his limitless power, and contemplates, in the unrestricted range of his infinite knowing, all that he has made, he must also love the things he creates, allowing them their autonomy and individuality, so as to delight in their multitudinous disparity. The Divine love is limitless; nothing other than God can impede or destroy it. It extends to all creatures impartially. While it is fairly absurd to speak of degrees of love, it is true that in loving all things without restriction, God's love is unsurpassable; no other love could extend so far and be so indefectible. The love of God is the concern to bring all things to their proper fulfilment, the fully sympathetic sharing in their interior passions of joy and sorrow, the giving of self-existent life, that it may return, at once diversified and enriched, to the primal unity of consciousness and content, in the all-encompassing reality of the Divine being.

Philosophers sometimes imagine a god who is omnipotent and omniscient, and yet totally without moral scruples, an arch-tyrant or amoral supreme being, who does not care for the world he creates, or perhaps only cares for his own pleasure, without regard for the good of creatures. Is such a being conceivable? What they have in mind is a being who takes pleasure in the sheer exercise of power, in showing its complete mastery over every other being. But, for God, there are no other beings except those he chooses to create; so there is nothing for him to demonstrate. A being who has un-surpassable power does not need to prove anything to him-self. Perhaps God could take pleasure in creating pain for others? But he is omniscient, so their pain must be included in his knowledge; it cannot be distanced from his own being. In fact, what such philosophers are thinking of is simply a very powerful being, but still a creature, which has goals of personal power yet to be achieved, and passions beyond rational control. The self-existent being, however, can have no power yet to be won, and no sheerly given, contingent, overwhelming passions which hold it helpless in its grip. God is necessarily what he is. If he creates objects, it is as a mani-festation of his own infinite being; their only purpose is, not to satiate his unfulfilled desire, but to express his positive creativity and contemplative delight.

If there is value in things at all — and that there is is a fundamental tenet of theism, without which it loses its rationale — then God, in knowing himself, will know that value. Even though it may be senseless to speak of a maxi-mum quantity of value, or a greatest possible sum of values, whatever God creates must be of value, and be created pre-cisely because it is of value. From all possible worlds, the omnipotent God chooses one which exhibits a unique range of values — or, perhaps, an endless number of worlds, each exhibiting one of the infinite possible combinations of value. God, by necessity of his nature, will choose what is worth while, because it is worth while. He will not choose it because it fills a need or lack in himself.

Yet surely, if God must create some world in order to express certain contingent features of his power and love, then he needs some world to be himself? One must here distinguish two senses of 'need', with respect to God. In one sense of need, a man may be said to need food and water if he is not to die. His need is a form of dependence on what is outside himself, and thus testifies to his contingency and weakness. If what he needs is not forthcoming from some source other than himself, he will cease to exist. What one needs is what one requires for existence, and it must be given from outside. To ascribe need in this sense to God has always been felt unacceptable and shocking to believers. Similarly, a desire is a wish for something one does not have, and which also needs to come from outside oneself. Desires may be frustrated, and are always to some extent a sign of dissatisfaction, of longing at the mercy of circumstance or difficult endeavour. When Dionysius speaks of the world as arising from the desire of God — 'a motion of desire simple, self-moved . . . overflowing from the Good into creation' (*On the Divine Names*, 4.14) — orthodox theism has drawn back in alarm, not wishing to ascribe any form of incompleteness or imperfection to God.

Orthodoxy has been quite right, in that God is essentially the self-existent and self-determining. His existence cannot depend upon any being outside himself; it is not contingent; his desires cannot be frustrated, and require no difficult endeavour; he cannot be dissatisfied with what he necessarily is. But if one is quite clear about that, one may proceed to speak of God as needing the universe, in a qualified sense. He needs it, in that he would not be completely what he is without it; though he need not have been just what he is in every respect. It depends on nothing other than him; his need cannot be frustrated; he does not have to wait for it to be met. If one insists that God might have created an amoral universe, not oriented to the realization of those personal values which are rooted in his own essential being, I suppose I would say that, if there are no objectively worthwhile states, then that could be so. But then the whole idea of creation as rational choice would disappear, and one would have to appeal to irrational desires of God as the only foundation of reality. If there are worthwhile states, then God will choose them, since he has no selfish or short-term desires which could conflict with such a choice. Men are selfish, because the goods they can have are in short supply, their lives are brief, and they are in constant competition with others. No such considerations are relevant for God. So, in choosing creativity and sensitivity for himself, in choosing their exercise as expressions of his personal perfection, he necessarily chooses them for any and all personal beings. For the almighty creator, goodness is not a scarce resource; it can therefore be shared with all created beings, without loss.

The spectre of the malignant demon fades, when it is seen that God is not just a powerful being who happens to have a certain nature, which could have been otherwise. God creates the world because he wants to. But why should God want a world? In order to exercise his power and knowledge. But what sort of objects will he exercise his power and knowledge upon? It must be remembered that God is self-explanatory, too; while he can create any possible world, the one he does create must be wholly explicable by reference to his nature. It is not sufficient to say that God chooses x just because he wants to, as if his want were a final, inexplicable given datum. His want, too, must be explicable; that he wants x rather than y must be explicable. What could explain it, except the fact that it possesses value, that it is worthy of choice by any rational being? Since God creates a world because it is of value, it would be irrational for him to seek to destroy that value. In this sense, the Thomist insight that evil is parasitic upon goodness, that it is a privation, not a positive reality, has force. For what God chooses to be must be good; that is why he chooses it. Destruction and loss are not directly willed by God; they cannot in themselves be objects of rational choice.

So God necessarily wills what is good; and chooses a unique set of goods from all possible goods which exist, as possibilities, in himself. Among all the possible goods there are, certain basic goods are defined by the nature of God as self-existent creator. If God chooses to create at all, he will necessarily develop his own power, knowledge and rational choice, precisely because these are basic values, and are thus worth developing in himself. So God will be creative, sensitive and beneficent; indeed, those properties are inextricable. Creation requires sensitivity to what is made, and beneficence to bring it into being. But God's power is uniquely such that the good things he creates and loves take on their own relative autonomy, and so enrich even the Divine being in a distinctive way, leading it from isolation to community. It adds a new dimension to the Aristotelian aristocrat to make incumbent upon it a real, developing relation with its own creatures. The creator of the world is necessarily, unsurpassably beneficent for he creates the world because it is good; all good things flow from him, and the standard of goodness is necessarily rooted in his eternal nature.

Thus the three basic Divine perfections are mutually entailing, as long as they are conceived as unlimited and necessarily possessed. Power entails omniscience and vice versa, while both together entail goodness, since God acts from perfect knowledge in virtue of the goodness of things. He is thus also perfectly wise and happy, for happiness lies in knowing and choosing the good. Goodness, in turn, if it is unlimited, entails omniscience; for one must know what is good in an unlimited way if one's goodness is to be unlimited; and so it entails omnipotence, too.

The fundamental presuppositions of this argument are that explicability and value are basic properties of the real. If the world is rational and valuable; if there is purpose achieved within limits of necessity, then there must exist a perfect being as its basis. In this chapter I have examined the notion of a perfect being. My conclusion has been that the idea of

God as including all properties in himself is incoherent, except in so far as this means that he contains the ideas of all things, and is the unconditioned ground of all reality. But a perfect being must be considered to be self-existent, and the five metaphysical, though formal, perfections of unity, immutability, aseity, necessity and completeness bring out what is implied by that notion. In traditional Christian theology, God has also been considered to be self-sufficient. I have argued that, to the extent that is true, almost nothing can be said of the nature of God, though perhaps happiness, consciousness, will and being must be ascribed to him. In any case, since God has created this world, he is not self-sufficient, but is related to creatures by way of the five personal perfections which define the maximization of rational choice — knowledge, power, goodness, wisdom and happiness. We can only conceive the objects of Divine knowledge as being the objects of this world. God's perfections are accordingly those which must be valued by any being which has reason to value anything in a world of finite evaluating agents; and they are maximally possessed, since they are, uniquely, directed to the whole of creation. The perfect being will possess all intrinsic values to a maximal degree; and will also possess the greatest set of actual values at every time. This definition is restricted, by comparison with that of Spinoza, who held that God is 'being absolutely infinite, that is to say, substance consisting of infinite attributes, each one of which expresses eternal and infinite essence' (*Ethics* 1). But we have seen that there are many attributes which God does not possess; and that the sense in which his attributes are unlimited needs to be carefully specified. Nevertheless, I think that one can make out a notion of a perfect being which is based on more than subjective preference, and that this being will be the one and only self-existent being, creator of everything other than itself.

But the major difficulty which remains is to give some coherent account of a God who seems to have split into two parts. By the axiom of intelligibility, we have a necessary, immutable, timeless individual as origin of all things. But by the doctrine of creation, we have a temporal, contingent and changing creative agent as the origin of all things. Plotinus' solution of making both these elements hypostases of the Divine Triad, flowing from an ineffable One, is tempting but little more than verbal in the end. The problem is precisely how the necessary can give rise to the contingent; and the word 'emanation' does not resolve that. It must now be seen if and how these two aspects of Godhood can be coherently held together, and what difference that makes to our view of the intelligibility, value and purposiveness of the universe. The final duality which rational theism must overcome, yet without dispensing with either part of it, is the fundamental duality of creation and necessity.

Time and Eternity

The classical definition of the eternity of God was given by
Boethius in his beautiful phrase, '*interminabilis vitae tota
simul et perfecta possessio*' — unending life existing as a complete whole all at once (*De Consolatione*, 5, 6). The life of
God, he says, is unending; it does not begin or cease to be,
and it exists completely as a whole (is perfectly possessed) all
at once. So it does not suffer the defects of temporal existence, which continually passes into non-being, which even in
the present is fleeting and temporary, which has a future uncertain and non-existent, and which does not possess at all its
past and its potential being. Yet at the same time, God does
have the advantages of temporal existence — a ceaseless or
even pure and perfect actuality of existence, so full that it
cannot pass away, and so great that it is present at every
actual and possible time. However, this striking phrase of
Boethius is in fact doubly contradictory. First, there is the
contradiction, noted by Anselm in *Monologion* 22, between
the claim that God must exist at every time (interminably)
and that he must exist wholly all at once, that is, either at
only one time or at no time at all. Second, there is the contradiction between the claim that God is timeless and the
claim that he perfectly possesses his being all at once, that is,
at one and the same time.

It may be said that what Boethius is trying to express is a
mode of existence which is beyond temporality in any sense
we experience it, but which is not simply the negation of
temporality altogether, and that such a heightened form of
temporality can only be expressed by paradox. I am sympa-

thetic to that proposal. On the other hand, if there are in fact no good religious or philosophical reasons for embracing these particular contradictions, and if a coherent account of God's eternity can be given without them, they can be abandoned without regret. What reasons are offered for supposing that God is eternal, in the sense of timeless, without temporal relation either within himself or to other things?

Anselm in the *Monologion,* offers three classical arguments, which go by way of immutability to timelessness. First, he argues that, if a being changes, it must either be changed by something other than itself, or by itself, or by nothing. If it is capable of being changed by something other than itself, then it cannot be omnipotent and must be subject to control or corruption. Further, the being, whatever it is, which changes it must be greater than it, in order to have the power to change it; so God would not be the greatest conceivable being, which is unpalatable. Second, change cannot come about through nothing, by the axiom of intelligibility; but even if it could, God could not change in that way, because he would then be subject to arbitrary and unpredictable changes, and might cease to possess some perfection, or to be the necessarily self-determining being, which is unacceptable. Third, Anselm holds that God cannot change himself; because the cause must precede its effect, and God cannot precede himself. Even if he could, there could not be an infinite series of causal states in God, for that would again make ultimate intelligibility impossible. So there must be one entirely unchanged state in God. Moreover, if God is perfect, any change must cause some perfection to cease or another perfection to come into being; but then he either would have been or will no longer be perfect, which is contradictory. Thus God must be immutable, and, since 'time is merely the numbering of before and after in change' (Aristotle, *Physics* 4, 2, 220a25), what cannot change cannot be in time.

The first argument is that God cannot be changed by anything other than himself. If God is the creator of all things, there can certainly be no opposing power, whether an evil power or a mere inertial power of matter, to restrict his will. All things exist by God's will. But, as has been suggested, God could freely create beings which are themselves free, in being self-determining, within the limits set by him. If this is conceivable, then even God cannot know in advance how they will choose, since the choice is undetermined. When they have chosen, God will know something that he could not have known before, the choices they freely make. In that way, God will be changed by something outside himself, a creature; but it by no means follows that the creature is greater than God, or that God is not omnipotent, even though he restricts the actual exercise of his power. No creature can cause God to lose his maximal knowledge or to be ignorant or misled, or can do what God does not permit. It is not a defect that God knows temporally; on the contrary, it involves the addition of a sort of property to God which he otherwise might have lacked. Even if it is said that God necessarily creates, and so necessarily limits the exercise of his power, that necessity arises solely from his own nature. The specific forms creation takes are still under his control, and he retains a directing and shaping power over it. Omnipotence is limited by love; but there is no imperfection about that. The ultimate fact remains that God, the ground of omnipotent love, cannot be destroyed or corrupted, but it is essential to his being love that he can be changed and affected by what his own power permits to be.

If genuinely free creatures are admitted, there is an overwhelmingly strong argument against Divine immutability and for Divine temporality. For the free acts of creatures will partially determine the initial conditions of the next temporal segment of the world. Before he creates that next segment, God must therefore know what choices have been made. The creation is consequent upon God's knowledge, which depends in turn upon free creaturely acts; so God must be conceived as responding to free acts moment by moment, as they are decided. It is useless to say, with Boethius, that God knows free acts non-temporally. For, given real freedom, God cannot complete his act of creation until he knows all the differences that the acts of creatures make to the initial conditions of various time-segments. One has a picture of God seeing all the choices of creatures, and then determining the whole world to take account of them, by a non-temporal act. But this picture is incoherent. Those free choices do not exist at all unless the world already exists up to that point in time; and once the world exists, one cannot subsequently change it by a non-temporal act — for to change it would be to cause it to cease to exist as the world that it is. The combination of non-temporal knowledge, non-temporal creation and free creaturely action is contradictory. For God's creation is consequent upon his knowledge, which depends in part on creaturely acts, which presuppose that creation has already taken place. The only break from this vicious circle is to conceive Divine creation as a gradual and temporal process, depending partly on possibilities in his own being and partly on creatures. In a strictly limited sense, God can be changed from without.

The second argument is that God cannot be changed through nothing. It is true that random change in God would be an imperfection. However, one may pause for a moment to consider whether there is any place for imaginative spontaneity in God. If he is called creator, by analogy with artists and dramatists, that would suggest that there is. Such creative spontaneity, which develops the familiar in new and unexpected ways, is not a case of random change, for it is mind-directed. Yet the creation is not somehow already there in the creator before it exists — a favourite model of philosophers from Plato and Augustine onwards. On the Greek and medieval Latin view of God, any effect must already exist in its cause, in an even higher manner. But that means that all effects are somehow already predetermined and utterly definite, and there can never be anything really new. All that ever is must always have been, in an even more real way. Creation can only be a sort of cosmic defect, whose only saving grace is that it leaves the supreme perfection of God completely untouched.

The model which is still working behind these ideas is that of the Platonic world of Forms, more real than the world of changing particulars, eternally specifying every possible state of affairs; 'before all things were made there was in the thought of the Supreme Nature what they were going to be' (*Monologion,* 9). All possibilities are eternally and exhaustively specified in the Divine nature. This sounds reasonable, for, if a thing is ever possible, surely it is always possible. That is, if it is ever true that x may be the case, then it must be always and immutably true that x may be the case, under suitably specified conditions. So God must know all possibles; and from them, he can select some world to actualize. Possibles cannot come into being or pass away. So, like God himself, they must be eternal and uncreated. It follows that they are not brought into being, even by God, but are parts of his immutable nature. God does not decide which possibles to create; all possibles are specified completely by the uncreated being of God himself.

The Augustinian move beyond the Platonic dualism of a world of Forms and the Demiurge whose intelligent acts were limited by the possibilities they presented to him, was to identify the Forms with the being of God, to make them ideas necessarily contained in the mind of the primal being. This eased the problem of what it could mean to speak of the actual existence of a mere possibility; for their actuality becomes that of the mind in which they inhere. It is no limitation on God to make ideas necessary to him; indeed, the alternative, which is to say that God is a completely undetermined will, is incoherent, and makes it impossible to distinguish between a rational act of choice and an arbitrary positing. God's will must be conditioned by his uncreated nature; he must have such a nature, and it is that nature which governs the sorts of possibles that necessarily exist.

Thus there are in the being of God himself the foundation of all rational principles and archetypes of possible goals, generated solely from himself by necessity of his nature. However, may there not be in God an element of creative spontaneity, so that he can freely generate new ideas, just as a human artist creates new tunes or patterns of colour? The archetypal world may not be immutably fixed; it may itself by modifiable by the creative intellect. Of course, the Divine intellect will not be able freely to generate every reality. It cannot, for instance, generate itself, its own necessarily possessed properties, or the most general archetypes of being which set the limits of any possible world — limits of goodness, intelligibility, beauty and purpose. But since, by the Augustinian revision of Platonism, ideas only have reality as contained in the Divine mind, once one is able to think of that mind as creative and mutable, a new perspective opens up.

As God is primarily a creative intellect, he can create new possibilities or develop and modify old ones. Thus there is no total sum of eternal ideas, but a constantly changing stock of imaginatively created ideas, limited only by God's character as wise, good and loving. This means admitting the strange-sounding axiom that new possibles can come into being. But if one is clear that possibles only exist in so far as they are conceived by the Divine mind, then it causes no difficulty that God should come to conceive new things — as long as he can change. All one has to say is that the future is truly open and undecided, even in thought. The creator will not only be ignorant of what will be actual in future, that he does not decree; he will not know everything that is possible. Nevertheless, this is by no means a defect in God; for if anything becomes possible, he alone makes it so, and this 'limitation' alone makes free creativity in God possible. To say that something is positively possible is to say that it is conceived by God, so he knows everything positively possible. Moreover, there is nothing else to know, since negative possibles (states of affairs which, when formulated, may well be not self-contradictory) do not exist at all. God is both the model of creation and the architect of the world, shaping it in accordance with his own nature, which he can, within limits, creatively change.

I am not only denying that the supreme being needs to contain in himself every possible perfection in a higher manner. I am also denying that God must conceive every possible world and state, immutably and exhaustively. Nevertheless, one wishes to exclude the possibility that things can simply come to be for no reason at all, in no intelligible relation to what already exists; for if this could happen, events in the world would be utterly unpredictable. Events must be related to their antecedents in ways which conform to rationally comprehensible patterns — embryos develop into humans by predictable processes, governed by physical laws. But it is not necessary that this process should be deterministic, in that, given the initial conditions and the set of laws, one could predict fully all that would ever occur, in principle. There is a place for statistical regularity which allows indeterminism within limits, and this may be held, not to diminish, but to increase, intelligibility. For reason, properly understood, is not simply a process of quasi-mechanical deduction. To be rational, in the fully human sense, is to be able to make connections, to advance to new creative insights, to see alternatives and judge between them and so on.

Thus, if our understanding of nature is to be taken as a rediscovery of God's rational creating of nature — as it must be for a theist — then we shall see nature to be more fully rational the less it is derivable deductively from first principles (as if God were simply a super-computer) and the more it is comprehensible as a product of creative insight and originality within a general structure of law. I propose that such a view gives more credit to God as a being of personal rationality, as a creator in the real sense, than the deterministic theories which can only view God as the sufficient cause of the world, determining all things as he must, with boring monotony. There is a place, then, for the indeterminate, the spontaneous, in an intelligible creation.

A possible analogy is that of a musical composition, where the harmonic possibilities and form are, in general, laid down by the cultural norms. New and surprising melodies nonetheless occur, which, if the composition is good, seem to develop intelligibly out of their thematic material, while still being works of individual genius, which not just anyone could manufacture. Analogously, what we need to understand causality is the general limits of necessity, laid down by physical laws, and also the genesis of new and surprising events which develop intelligibly from their antecedents without being strictly deducible from them. That, I suggest, is the sort of causal order one would expect if there were a personal creator of the world.

If this is so, one must reject the claim that any perfection must be found in its cause; but one is not thereby committed to saying that perfections come into being from nowhere, irrationally or arbitrarily. New perfections come into being within patterns of general law and are generated by imaginative transformation from antecedent data. It is hard to imagine how properties can be genuinely new and emergent, but the notion of creation must be a mystery on any account, and it is perhaps even harder to suppose that everything that comes to be must already have existed, and so there could never be anything new at all. The ultimate presupposition of the intelligibility of the world turns out to be not that it necessarily follows by the principle of sufficient reason from an *ens realissimum*, but that it is structured by an ordering and inventive mind. In this limited sense, God's creative acts are not sufficiently determined, even by his own nature; they are free and spontaneous, within the more general limits of necessity rooted in his nature. That is, God can be changed through nothing, in that many of his particular acts are not sufficiently determined by anything, even though they are all necessarily caused by him.

The third argument is that God cannot change himself. This is partly because he would then have to precede himself. But we have seen that it is consistent to suppose that some states of God do precede others. However, the intelligibility arguments for God claim to have established that there must be an unchanged cause of all change. Therefore there cannot be an infinite series of self-caused changes in God, or explanation will always be incomplete. At every stage, one will have to explain the actual state of God by referring to a previous state; and if this goes on infinitely, explanation will never end. On the other hand, if there is a beginning of change in God, then one has to think of him as becoming temporal at a certain point. But then there was a time when God was changeless, followed by a time at which he changed, which contradicts the hypothesis. If one says that God did not exist *before* he began to change — that is, apart from change he only exists timelessly, and therefore not in any temporal relation to any time — then he must be totally immutable in that eternal state. And so one is back to the impossibility of such a being producing a contingent world of free creatures. The dilemma seems unavoidable: either there is no complete explanation of the world or there is no free and creative action.

We have already renounced some of the requirements for intelligibility which the Greeks and medievals generally thought necessary, including the idea of metaphysical perfection and of Divine self-sufficiency. Can we go further still, and renounce the impossibility of an infinite regress of explanations in time, without undermining intelligibility altogether? In speaking of an infinite regress, Aquinas says, 'an infinite series of efficient causes essentially subordinate to one another is impossible . . . all the same an infinite series of efficient causes incidentally subordinate to one another is not counted impossible' (*Summa Theologiae,* qu. 46, art. 2). The point is rather obscure, but appears to be that, if A happens to have a particular cause, but did not need to have it to be what it is, that cause is irrelevant to a complete explanation of A's action or state. Thus, although every state may have been caused by a preceding state, on the hypothesis that time is infinite, it is not necessarily so, and could have been directly caused by Divine decree. The preceding cause, though real enough, did not have to exist, while the causality of God is essential; the state could exist without the former, but not without the latter.

If God freely causes the first state of the universe, no sufficient explanation of it is possible; there can only be a reference to God's free choice. Suppose that God is, by necessity of his nature, the unsurpassably powerful and knowing creator. It will follow that any world he creates must possess certain characteristics — perhaps, that it must actualize the creative, communal pursuit of goals by creatures. But the exact nature of that world is unspecifiable from knowledge of his nature alone. That does not mean that it is simply arbitrary; it means that it results from an act of creative choice, which is itself necessary in its general nature though not its specific detail.

If one can offer that form of explanation for a first state of the universe, one can equally well offer it for any state of the universe. The only difference is that, if time is infinite, each state will refer back in time to an infinite number of past states, though it could have been directly produced by God without such a reference. The appeal of a first temporal state is illusory, since it leaves one with a set of actual conditions and general laws which depend on the Divine will. Once total necessitarianism has been abandoned, one can only account for the initial state by referring to such rational considerations as that it is an efficient means to the attainment of some freely chosen purpose, which expresses the Divine nature as necessarily creative. But one can equally well give this form of explanation for every temporal state; there is no reason why the Divine purposes should be finite. Indeed, if God is truly infinite, there is every reason to think that his purposes are infinite, and that God is characterized by an unlimited self-creative activity. Ironically, the very biblical text which Aquinas appealed to in support of the view that God was changeless — 'I am that I am' (Exod. 3) — provides even better support for the view that God is unlimitedly potential and therefore ceaselessly changing. For an equally good translation, and one more sympathetic to Hebrew thought forms, would be, 'I will be what I will be'; so the words would explicitly refer to the dynamic potency of the Divine as its central characteristic.

When some specific Divine purpose is in process of being actualized, then a reference to past states is essential to explanation; for one needs to see both the starting-point and the goal to understand a purposive process fully. Though God could have created this universe five seconds ago, with all its developed complexity, its nature as a developing and partially self-creating unity suggests its derivation from simpler inorganic states by a process of law-governed emergence. So, to understand it, we need to retrace that process to its simplest beginnings. But there is no reason why the beginning of this universe, in this phase of its existence, should be the beginning of God's purposes or his only arena of activity. The purposes of God may well be endless, and all explained as free expressions of his changeless nature, changeless in being the one self-determining, almighty and self-giving creator.

One still has a reference, in explanation, to a necessary, immutable being who is the cause of all, and it is true that without any such reference the world would remain ultimately unintelligible. But it now becomes clear that these properties are true of God only in certain respects: that is, he is not wholly immutable and necessary, for he is also changing and contingent. Before one leaps to accusations of self-contradiction, however, one should recall that assertions are only contradictory if they attribute contradictory properties to something at the same time, and in the same respects. God is not immutable in the same respects as those in which he is creative and therefore changing. What cannot be changed is that God is the sole creator; what changes is the way in which he expresses this creative activity. One might say that God timelessly generates, by the necessity of his own nature, the infinite series of temporal states in which he freely acts.

If this is so, it is easily seen why so many writers speak of an impersonal Godhead beyond the personal God — Brahman behind Brahma in the Indian tradition, the One beyond Intellect in Plotinus. But it must be stressed that, if generation is spoken of here, it is timeless. Also that, since it is necessary generation, God would not be God without his temporal, personal aspect; he never exists without it. So one is in no sense ascending to a truer view of God by transcending the personal will and discovering the necessary Absolute. One is uncovering the finally explanatory element in God, but all aspects of the Divine are necessary to his being what he is.

I conclude that there can be an infinite series of Divine states, such that no explanatory terminus can be found within them. But the whole remains intelligible by being seen as the expression of a nature which is itself necessary and changeless. The final vindication of this view lies in the fact that God could not possess the necessary properties he does, unless he also possessed various contingent properties. Aquinas dimly saw this point when he insisted that God, though by his arguments he should have been the simple abstract Form of Being, was in fact the most ceaselessly active of all beings. But it is precisely that notion of activity which Thomism cannot in the end allow for. The idea of perfection which is used is that of something static, which cannot change on pain of becoming worse. So the Thomist God must be both immutable and supremely active at the same time, a feat beyond even the capacity of omnipotence.

Once the idea of metaphysical perfection has been rejected, why should one insist that any perfect being cannot change without getting worse? If it is a perfection — a good thing — to be creative, that entails change. Omnipotence, taken in any straightforward sense, entails the ability to do things, and thus the possession of capacities which may be actualized, but can only be so by active change. Goodness, too, if it is not interpreted as the possession of every possible property, is most naturally seen as entailing specific acts of beneficence or love, which will change in accordance with circumstances. Thus again, in some respects God cannot change without getting worse — in his possession of omnipotence, goodness, omniscience and happiness, perhaps. But these properties, properly understood, entail changes of specific state, in which there is no question of better or worse involved. Once one drops the incoherent notion of metaphysical perfection as the actual possession of the maximal degree of every possible property, and replaces it with the notion of evaluative perfection, of what it is preferable to possess, then most changes in God lead to the existence of states which are neither better nor worse than their predecessors. God's evaluative perfections are changeless; but they by no means range over all the properties he possesses, so that many possibilities of change, indeed, an infinite number, exist in God. This conception allows a much more satisfactory interpretation of Divine omnipotence, not as the actual performance of everything he could do, but as infinite potency, by which God is the creative ground of unlimited possible goals.

Anselm's arguments for the necessary immutability of a perfect being all fail, and it becomes clear that traditional Christian concepts of God have stressed his intelligibility at the expense of his creativity. Yet hesitation may still be felt about ascribing change, and hence temporality, to God. Paul Tillich protests that such views subject God to the power of fate, the anarchy of non-being which threatens from a future which is not-yet, or from a past which is always falling into nothingness (*Systematic Theology*, vol. 1. ch. 11). God must be time-transcending, in that he is not externally limited by time, or under the independent power of time. I think Tillich's charge is unfair, though it is true that Whitehead does refer to God as the 'first creature', as subordinate to Creativity. Suppose, though, that the past does not become non-existent, but is always perfectly retained in being — in the memory of God, which is perfect, total and indestructible. That conception, which Whitehead calls 'objective immortality', seems to me intelligible, or not less so than most suppositions at this remote level. This would give God the sort of time-transcending knowledge of the past which traditional theists have given him of all time. The point is, however, that such knowledge is only possible when there is no creative freedom left. So while it is possible to have such knowledge of the past, it is not possible to have it of any future in which there is creative freedom.

Does that entail that the future is not completely under the control of God, since it does not yet exist? The appeal to timelessness can give an illusion of control here, but it can be easily seen through. The illusion is that what is future to us can be controlled by God because it is not future to him. Far from time limiting God, he wholly creates it, past and future as it is to us, and everything in it. But this is an illusion. For, just as it could be necessary for God to exist timelessly, so it can equally easily be necessary for him to exist at every time, and to have full control over every possible future time. It is not simply the fact that God knows all time as present that makes him omnipotent; and, in fact, timelessness adds nothing to his power or his necessity. What does not yet exist can be necessarily under God's control. As Anselm rightly said, if God is good, he cannot willingly cease to be; and if God is omnipotent, he cannot unwillingly cease to be. So he is everlasting, and his necessary nature at each moment of change controls what shall be in the next moment. Timelessness does not give God a special sort of control over the future unobtainable in any other way. It is the necessity of Divine omnipotence which guarantees his complete control over the future; the non-existence of the future can pose no threat to such an unlimited power.

Nevertheless, the view I am proposing does carry the consequence that there are times at which God exists. This in turn entails that God does not create those times; he cannot logically create a condition of his own existing. Time becomes a property of God, rather than something he creates. Is this a limitation on the being of God? One has the image of temporality as a sort of abstract universal, independent of God and limiting his unrestricted being. But we have seen that such universals are necessarily parts of the being of God, not at all independent of him. Temporality is a necessary property of God, a property he could not fail to possess, being what he is. Is the possession of such properties a limitation?

There is a sense in which temporality limits God, for it is a specific way in which he exists, so that his being cannot be completely unrestricted or unconditioned. But the notion of 'unrestricted existence', of existence which has no specific characteristics, is in any case unintelligible. God has the properties of omnipotence, omniscience and goodness; these are ways in which he exists, they depend on nothing outside himself, and belong to him of necessity. To possess such properties is no defect, but a condition of being the unsurpassably perfect being. God creates the space-time in which we exist, just as he maintains in being our good acts. But he himself possesses temporality as an uncreated and necessary property, which is a condition of his uniquely originative creativity. If this is a limitation, it is one which is necessary to God being what he is, and which in no way detracts from the evaluative perfection of his being.

To ask how the time of God relates to human time is to ask how the life of God relates to human life. Put in that way, the question is unanswerable, since no one has access to the inner life of God. But we must certainly think of God, as he is in relation to us, as contemporary with every present.

To that extent, we must think of the Divine time as running in parallel with human time; only in that way can he hear and respond to prayer or act causally to produce new effects in the world. This does, however, raise a difficulty which is highlighted by the theory of relativity. According to that theory, there is no such thing as absolute simultaneity; one is not permitted to say that two events very far removed from each other in space are, or are not, absolutely simultaneous. All observations of simultaneity are relative to the observer; so it does not make sense to think of time as one absolute medium within which all cosmic events can be given a place, relative to each other. Thus it seems that one cannot say that God is simultaneous with all events in the universe at a given time, since there is no such absolute time.

So when speaking of God as temporal, I mean in no way to deny that he surpasses time, or to assert that the Divine life is successive in just the way that ours is. What I want to affirm is that we can speak correctly of God, though only as he exists in relation to us. In this respect, it is correct to say that God is temporal, in being the creator and final cause of our universe, and as being temporally related to us as creatures. Whatever we signify by eternity, we cannot contradict that truth. But if we then go on to say that God unimaginably surpasses this temporality, that we can see the deficiency in saying that he possesses temporality as we do, that perhaps all our concepts are inadequate to express the Divine being adequately; all that must be gladly admitted. It must be far from the mind of any theist to think that he can encompass in thought the majesty of the self-existent ground of all beings. But it is important, too, that what we can say of God should be consonant with the highest insights of reason, and should be both coherent and true. And that, when we have reached the place where human thought can proceed no further, when we are sure that place is not merely a mirage of human ignorance, then we must cease speaking.

We are now in a position to see how the idea of a necessary, immutable, eternal individual, the ground of rationality, can be coherently combined with the idea of a temporal creator, the ground of freedom and contingency. The general solution is to say that there is just one individual, possessing both a set of necessary properties and a set of contingent properties. God is changeless in at least these ways: he is the sole self-determining being; he knows all conceived possibles and all actuals; he has power unlimited by anything other than himself; he is supremely good. He also contains within his being certain necessary, immutable archetypes of any possible creation; these set the limits of all possible words, though they are not exhaustively specified to cover every actual eventuality. They will include patterns of rationality and moral ideals as well as specifications of descriptive properties.

All these properties, being changeless, are eternal in the sense of being timeless, and they are in themselves uncaused, uncausing and unconscious. That they are uncaused follows immediately from the underivability of the Divine nature. That they are uncausing may seem more surprising. Was the whole argument to an immutable being precisely not a search for a first cause? It was; but the search ended by the discovery that an immutable cause must be necessary, so whatever such a cause produces must itself be (dependently) necessary. Any cause of contingent entities must itself be contingent, since its causal acts could be other than they are. Thus what is required, as the cause of a contingent but intelligible world, is a contingent cause working in accordance with necessary principles, or having a nature in some respects necessary. The eternal archetypes, the Forms, are not themselves causes, since the realities in which they instantiated are contingent. They are used as models for actualizing entities; they necessarily limit the activity of the causal power, being parts of his nature.

This leads one to say that, if God's time is contemporary with the time of every creature, and if all creatures cannot be located in one time-stream, relative to each other, God must exist in a number of different time-sequences, not relatable to each other by relations of absolute simultaneity. This is certainly a surprise for common sense, as most conclusions of modern physics seem to be. But it is not incoherent. It is just a particular case of the truth that God can create different universes, different space-time systems, which cannot be spatially or temporally related to one another. He will relate himself to each of those systems, in such a way that he will exist simultaneously with each event in each system, as it occurs. But those different time sequences will not be temporally relatable to each other; one will not be able to say that events in one universe exist before or after events in another, even from God's point of view. This is difficult to imagine, but easy to conceive. For if time is a certain sort of relation — of before and after — between events, it is clearly logically possible to have sets of events related by that relation, but not related by it to other similar sets of events. Just as God may be said to be in every space, though also to be not confined to space or located in space in a bodily way, so he may be said to be present at every created time, though not confined to it.

We may conceive the situation thus: God is temporal, in that he does some things before he does others; and, in changing, he projects his being along one continuous temporal path. But there may be many such paths, either in different universes, or within one relativistic universe, which are not absolutely correlatable with each other. So God must be conceived as moving along all such paths, as existing in a number of different times. To the extent that this is so, there cannot be causal relations between those times, for each such point of correlation would establish a simultaneity. We may speak of God, then, not just as temporal, but as multi-temporal. One and the same self-existent perfect being may exist in a number of non-temporally related times. This certainly adds another dimension to our thinking of God as everlasting; and it gives added force to speaking of God as eternal, in the sense, not of being timeless, but of surpassing time, while including it. We are not only to think of God as beginning this universe, with some primeval big bang, and as bringing it to some future consummation, when it ends. Nor are we only to think of God as generating this universe end- lessly. Our horizons expand dramatically and unimaginably, as we think of an infinity of universes, beyond any temporal relation to us, and of an infinity of creatures, realizing end- less sets of purposes.

The limits of rational theology verge on fantasy, and, as our normal concepts begin to break and fall away, we find ourselves in a logical vacuum where reason and imagination become confused. But one might think of the testimony of most religions to the existence of the 'hosts of heaven', the spiritual beings who inhabit the courts of the presence of God, the angels and archangels who reflect the Divine glory. And one might be released from the constant temptation of making God too small, so that he comfortably fits our con- cepts. When one comes to the borderland of fantasy, it is better to be silent, but one can recognize that it is not the silence of simple self-contradiction and incoherence. It is the silence of wisdom, seeing that the demands of reason lead us first to speak of God and then to bow before his incompre- hensibility.

The immutable properties of God are not causes, since they are abstract properties, and only actual entities can be causes. Thus the property of being necessarily omnipotent is the property of 'being more powerful than any other possible being'. But such a property is not a cause of anything, though it states something about an entity which is a cause; it par- tially specifies the nature of a causal agent. The point here is the very simple one that properties are not causes; only in- dividual agents are. So the first cause of the universe must be an individual agent. Since this universe is contingent, the first cause must be contingent in its particular causal action. But since the general nature of this universe is necessary, the acts of the first cause must be governed by necessary aspects of its nature (by its necessary properties). Thus, though God's necessary properties are not causal, they limit or specify the sorts of causal acts he performs. They are parts of God and, though not themselves conscious, being abstract, they are objects of his everlasting consciousness. They are timeless, in the sense that they have no internal temporal relations (though awareness of them must be conceived as having duration, and they never exist unconceived). There are, then, timeless aspects of God's being, everlastingly known by him. But from the eternal alone, no causal power flows. The eternal is revealed by a consistent theism as being, not a separate impersonal being, but an impersonal aspect of the being of the everlasting God, an object of his incorruptible awareness and the foundation and archetype of all created beings.

An analogy may be found in the relation of the human mind's dispositions to its particular acts. If a man is loving, then we may say that his character determines that, in general, whatever acts he does will be of a certain sort. But the particular acts which express his love will be freely decided by actual temporal choices, underivable in detail from a knowledge of his character alone. Character is here the analogue of God's eternal nature; but in the case of God, that nature is necessary and without any possible occasions of acting out of character. It is fully known to him and sets limits to his specific acts throughout every possible change of his states. If one considers the eternal properties of God in isolation, one derives the impersonal concept of God as the Ideal, the Good, the timeless source of obligation, rationality and possibility. If one considers the temporal properties of God in isolation, one derives the personal concept of God as a loving Father who cares for all his creatures. But when one conceives of God in these two ways, one is not thinking of two distinct beings, or even of two separate hypostases within one Divine nature. An agent without a determinate nature is inconceivable. But the nature is not that which acts; it is precisely the nature of that which acts, of the agent. There are not two beings, a nature and an agent, but one, an agent with awareness, purpose and creative power, possessed of an immutable nature.

The ascription of temporality to God is not the subjection of the Divine to an alien power of fate. God is time-transcending, in that all past time is perfectly preserved in him; all possibilities are fully known by him and the future goal of creation is assured by his omnipotence and immutable love. Time is not an independent power which forces him along its path however unwillingly; it is his own creative will projecting change and freedom into the future. And the future is not an abyss of arbitrary freedom or chaos of non-being; at each moment it is under the control of God's omnipotent will. Both creative freedom and total control are coherently united in the one concept of God as temporal awareness and purposive will. The ancient tension between intelligence and necessity, freedom and rationality, is resolved.

The ascription of temporality to God drives out for ever the spectre of deism. For creation is seen, not as an arbitrary, once-for-all bringing to be, followed by aeons of masterly inactivity, nor as a timeless act which leaves God completely unchanged and unaffected by anything that happens in creation, but as a continually renewed expression of the primal creativity of an essentially self-determining and purposive God. We can treasure Boethius' phrase, except for the '*tota simul*', which is the source of all the contradictions so tempting to subsequent theologians, so destructive of clarity and coherence in theology. God remains the possessor of time without beginning or end, of 'unending life, perfectly possessed'; but he also is a being who communicates that life freely to an infinity of creatures, which are modelled on archetypal ideals necessarily grounded in his immutable nature.

There is, then, a coherent notion of a perfect creator, a

being which is self-explanatory within the limits which the
existence of freedom places on all rational explanation,
namely, that not everything about him can logically be explained in terms of the principle of sufficient reason. It is the
value of freedom which makes this restriction necessary and
desirable. In order to understand this value more fully, and
the way in which it relates to the human sense of moral
obligation, we must next turn to ask how the creative freedom of God and the moral freedom of humanity together
form a coherent whole of unique value and explanatory
power.

8   The Goodness of God

The quest of rational theism is the quest for that which fully explains being. One way of obtaining such a complete explanation is to provide a sufficient reason for the existence of the world, by the postulate of a self-explanatory and wholly necessary being. While that has been the constant temptation of rationalist philosophers, its consequence is to render freedom and contingency impossible. Since they are features of the world, explanation in terms of sufficient reason must be abandoned as insufficient. The alternative, which seemed too naive and subjective at first, but which turns out to be an essential complement to the rationalist vision, is to explain events in terms of the purpose and free choice of a rational being. Once one accepts the idea of a temporal, everlasting God, one is committed to explaining the finite world, partly as governed in its existence and structure by his necessary nature, and partly as expressing his freely chosen purposes.

When the notion of purpose was considered in chapter 5, it was pointed out that one can only consider a process as purposive if it culminates in or expresses a state or process which is considered to be of value. The ideas of purpose and value necessarily imply one another, in that, if any rational being has some purpose, he must consider it as productive of value; and if he considers something to be a value, he will, other things being equal, pursue it. Thus, if one considers the world to be expressive of the purposes of God, one must also consider it to be expressive of his values. For a full and adequate explanation of a contingent universe, one needs to employ the concepts of necessity, purpose and value. Without necessity, values would be arbitrary and inexplicable; without value, necessity would be blind and pointless; without purpose, both would be immobile and unproductive.

One cannot satisfactorily ground the finite universe in a God whose values are wholly contingent, like Calvin's God, who could choose anything at all as a value, at the fiat of his arbitrary will. That would be repugnant to our sense of moral importance, and would fail to note that the Divine choices are rooted in necessities of his nature. Nor can we ground it in a being without value, like Spinoza's God, who necessarily produces all possible beings because he has no alternative. That would totally ignore our sense of moral freedom, and would fail to note that our search for intelligibility is also a search for meaning, for what gives point to existence. To arrive simply at necessity without value would undermine our hope of finding some reality which would be self-justifying by being of absolute and unsurpassable value. And one cannot ground the universe in a God without purpose for the world, like Aristotle's God, who contemplates his own perfection for eternity. That would eradicate the point of any practical activity, and would make the existence of a finite world unintelligible.

In short, our quest for intelligibility is not a purely theoretical enterprise, as though theism was primarily an exercise in something like pure mathematics, enjoyable though that is for some. It is also a matter of practical concern, calculated to suggest an answer to the questions 'What should I, as a rational agent, do?' and 'What may I hope for, as the goal of my action?' The very form of the questions rules out the appeal to necessity which satisfies the purely speculative quest. It shows that any possible adequate answer must be in terms of values which can direct action to worthwhile goals. When we, as practical and free agents, ask, 'Why is the universe as it is?', we require not only the backward-looking appeal to the necessary structures of any and all being, but also the forward-looking vision of a goal which will be intrinsically worthwhile. The theist therefore introduces the concept of God both as the foundation of the ultimate importance of free moral action, and as the guarantor of a future goal which will be of absolute value.

Naturally, as in the speculative case, it cannot be established beyond reasonable doubt to any impartial spectator that such a form of explanation will be forthcoming and exemplified in reality. But, just as the possibility of total explanation may be thought to be presupposed both in common sense and in scientific activity, so the possibility of a final teleological explanation may be said to be presupposed in moral commitment and the basic conviction of an ultimate unity of reason and moral endeavour.

This is the sort of argument that Kant tried to develop in the *Second Critique,* though his version of it is notoriously unsatisfactory. Having argued that one must be unconditionally committed to morality, whether or not one believes in God, he goes on to say that one must believe that there will be an ultimate coincidence of virtue and happiness, if one is not to lose all motivation to moral action. Since it is obvious that no such thing happens in this world, one must postulate both immortality and a God who can guarantee the desired connection. Most commentators have simply jettisoned all Kant's talk about a *'summum bonum'* as unjustifiable, and stressed the categorical nature of moral obligation as his chief contribution to ethics. But, however weak Kant's specific arguments are, it is of decisive importance for his whole outlook that morality is a product of practical *reason,* not of feeling or of any external authority. Practical and speculative reason are not completely divorced, and Kant's main concern is to hold that, however much the claims of morality must be immune from purely speculative criticism, they do emanate from reason. It is very far from Kant's mind to make morality into a series of unconditional and arbitrary commands, which one must obey without question. On the contrary, morality is just reason expressed in action, and thus it cannot come into conflict with the necessary demands of speculative reason, but must have an intelligible place in the rational scheme of the world. It is, he holds, a requirement of the rationality of morals that virtue is not just pointless, but eventually correlates with happiness.

Kant explicitly distinguishes his view from the two extremes of what he calls Epicurean and Stoic ethics. For Epicurean ethics, morality is a matter of doing what brings long-term happiness, what is in one's own best interests, what one really wants. That view, he protests, misses the rigour and overridingness of moral claims, which often seem to ignore all our interests and lead to acts of self-sacrifice and self-denial. It is no use asking what I want in the long term, when some moral obligation simply confronts me and requires my submission. I ought to be truthful, loyal and just, whatever I may or may not want. Such total commitments give the highest worth to human life; they can only be weakened by raising questions of my desires.

For Stoic ethics, on the other hand, morality is a matter of doing my duty simply for its own sake, without regard to happiness or consequences. That view, Kant objects, is fanatical and irrational, for human action must have some relation to what brings happiness, and must be aimed at some ends. In so far as morality seeks to answer the question 'What is a reasonable way for me to act?', it must refer to my desires, to what I intend and wish for. It would be absurd to do something just because it was right, as though that had no relation to the nature and fundamental dispositions of the choosing agent. (The fact that some people think this was Kant's view shows how much they have misunderstood him.)

Morality, then, must both be a matter of overriding importance on its own account, and must possess some necessary relation to human nature and inclination. We cannot answer a moral question by considering the question 'What will make me most happy?', for actual human nature is so diverse and changeable that the answers will vary enormously.

In any case, as is well known by those who have had the opportunity, the pursuit of happiness is basically unsatisfying without a sense of the worthwhileness of what one is pursuing. Animal contentment is not what we seek, but some worthwhile goals which will bring happiness as a by-product of their pursuit. No goal will be worthwhile if it does not bring happiness to someone; but that happiness is only one element in the conceived end.

It seems to me that this notion of 'worth' or 'value' is ineliminable and not reducible to any other notion. Morality does not consist of a set of absolute duties which have no relation to human nature or happiness, but nor is it reducible to considerations either of how men naturally tend to act or of what they basically desire. If one looks at how men naturally tend to act one may well conclude that, while they have in common some desire to survive, to avoid injury, to have some companionship and to be happy, they also have fairly evident desires to kill and enslave each other, to fight, compete and generally despise each other. It is just begging the question to say that the former set of inclinations are those which are most natural, and therefore moral. It is arguably the latter, in a context of the principle of the survival of the fittest, which are most natural, while the former are the anaemic virtues of the timid and weak. What is the principle upon which some desires are selected as most natural? In fact, it is usually a shadow cast by some abandoned religious view, long ago deprived of its force and appeal, and accordingly reduced from an imperious command to the status of a hypothetical dream.

What the secular moralist has given up is the belief that man has been created by a purposive God, so that he has a basic and proper nature: the nature which God intends him to have, the archetype of human perfection which eternally exists in the Divine mind. For the theistic view, the 'natural' desires are those which are consonant with the purpose of God, with the nature of man as Divinely intended. They are both necessarily rooted in the Divine nature, and commanded by the active will of God to be nurtured and developed. It is usually these same desires which the liberal secular moralist espouses. But without a God to give them objective validity and overriding authority, they are transmuted into the sorts of desires that one would choose in the purely hypothetical situation where one was a fully rational agent among others. The view is quite unable to cope with a complex reality in which no one is fully rational, and the hypothetical comes to seem impossibly idealistic in fact. All that is left is return to the absurdity of moral commitment in an amoral universe (the Stoic view) or the sort of compromise with reality which makes morality a mere dream of what might have been.

I believe that Kant correctly perceived, but curiously misstated, the situation when he asserted that it is essential to preserve the overriding claims of morality, but that it is irrational to do so if morality is not somehow rooted in the nature of things, so that it connects with rational necessity and natural purpose within one intelligible whole. Morality must connect with rational necessity, because its demands cannot be arbitrary or contingent; what is right could not possibly have been wrong, Calvin notwithstanding. Morality must connect with natural purpose, because it must be concerned with what it is proper for man to be, with a fulfilment of human nature, with the performance of acts which are expressive of true humanity. All these terms presuppose that there is a true and proper form of human nature, that it is purposively constituted towards a specific fulfilment, and the moral way lies in the attainment of this purpose. However, morality is not reducible to either necessity or purpose. What is necessary need not be good, and what fulfils human nature may be without intrinsic value.

This non-reducibility of value is what those have in mind who protest that it does not help the cause of morality to make it depend upon the will of God. For, they ask, why should one obey God's will? If it is just because he is powerful, that is obedience out of fear; but if it is because he is good, then goodness does not depend on God after all, and he is irrelevant to morality. However, it should now be clear that, though God is good, and therefore does possess the property of goodness, that property is not something independent of God, which limits him in an undesirable way. It is a necessary part of the being of God, and could not exist as necessary in isolation from the totality of the Divine nature. Things are not therefore good, independently of God, any more than they are powerful, independently of God. All finite goods are brought about solely by God; and God is such that he will only bring about things which are good, or instrumental to or consequential upon things which are good. The reason why God should be obeyed, then, is that God, by the necessity of his immutable nature, wills only what is good; so in obeying him one is aiming at the good for its own sake.

But in that case, does God make any difference to morality at all? I believe that he makes the most important difference of all, in that only the existence of God can give morality an objective foundation and intelligible fulfilment. One may ask what gives morality its overriding importance. Here, it seems to me essential to maintain that moral statements are truth-valued. They are not expressions of feeling or prescriptions which we invent. One can discover moral truths or be mistaken about them, develop moral insight towards a truer perception, or become blind to their claims. It is true that torture is wrong, whether or not anyone believes it. What makes such statements true is not any fact about human minds or desires, but some fact which is objective and necessary, since moral truths are true by necessity. Moreover, such truths are not simply descriptive; they place a claim upon the actions of rational beings. Rather like the laws of logic, they state what can or cannot be done; they are action-guiding.

Human beings can resist such action-guiding force, because of inertia, ignorance, self-centredness or passion. There are other forces in the human disposition which may counteract moral directives, and when they do, those directives are felt as obligations, with that unique quality of constraint which produces guilt and repentance. The sense of guilt arises, when it is rational, because one did not do something that was within one's power, or did something one need not have done, in opposition to one's sense of how a human being ought to act, of what is proper to one as man. Such ideal patterns of human behaviour can themselves be perverse, as in the restricted honour-codes of many tribal societies. But at their worst they still testify obscurely to a sense of there being a true way of living as a man, and therefore to a sense of what human nature essentially is.

God, being necessarily what he is, cannot be subject to obligation or capable of sin. But human nature is contingent, and is able either to shape itself according to an ideal pattern or, by insisting on its own autonomy, refuse to do so. In God, the ideal is actual; the way he ought to be is the way he is; and, being necessarily so, it does not obligate him. In humanity, the ideal appears as obligation, because there are so many paths which tempt one away from actualizing it. In the abstract, one can see what values are intrinsic; the argument for this was rehearsed in chapter 5, where it was argued that any free finite sentient being must take creativity, sensitivity, happiness and love as basic values. Any state in which these values were maximized, so as to produce a community of sentient beings freely pursuing all permissible purposes co-operatively, would be of intrinsic value.

In the abstract, it is not difficult to perceive this ideal. What is difficult is to see whether and how it has any application in the actual world. Where striving often entails suffering and defeat; where the strong oppress the weak; where the weak admire the ruthless; in such a world the ideal can become so hypothetical as to lose all practical force. It is overwhelmingly apparent that this world is far from ideal, that injustice and war and starvation are great and self-perpetuating evils. Yet we do live in such a world, so why should some abstract propositions, which would be action-guiding in a non-existent ideal world, have any force at all?

This is where it is important that the ideal is rooted in some objective reality, and is not just an impractical dream. For an atheist, there is no objective purpose in the history of the universe or the existence of humanity; there is no objective value which is set before humanity as a possible goal, to be achieved by striving and self-mastery. One exists by chance; and nothing besides oneself determines the course of life one should try to take in the world; nor is there any enduring goal for which one may reasonably hope; all goals, all good and evil alike, will perish in the same unconscious, unguided, uncaring cosmic immensity. It is not surprising if a person who has such beliefs — and they may be true — rejects the ideal dream in favour of more palatable and immediate goals of his own contrivance. He can still care about the sufferings of others and work to alleviate them. What it would be irrational for him to do would be to commit his life wholly to the pursuit of an ideal as in any way a 'true' goal of human life.

Those who hold that moral assertions are truth-valued may say that there are objective and necessary facts which make them true, and which guide action because they state an objective ideal of human nature. The clearest model of this situation is the Platonic one of eternal archetypes of human nature, which define what it is to live in accordance with one's essential nature as human. If one adopts the view I have suggested of placing such Ideals in the Divine mind, then one can say that 'God is good' in the sense that the necessary archetypal Ideas which are parts of his eternal nature define what human goodness is. Perhaps this is what the scholastics intended when they said that God was not only good, but was 'goodness itself': that is, while intrinsic values are necessarily what they are, and are not reducible to non-evaluative concepts, they are necessary parts of the Divine nature; and as such, they comprise the standard of all human goodness, and set the possible limits of all Divine action.

Still, it may be said, even if there is an objective ideal of human action, if it does not necessarily guide our acts, why should we permit it to do so? One fairly uninformative answer is that one simply ought to, but one does have to spell that out a little to avoid the impression of sheer arbitrariness. One may say that thereby humanity achieves its objectively intended realization – remembering that value is not being reduced to purpose, but is being located in a context of purpose, so as to show that it is not arbitrary. We are supposing that we all agree what values are, and that they are values, things worth aiming at for their own sake, other things being equal. This bare supposition, that something is worth aiming at for its own sake, already implies objective moral truth, regardless of our actual desires and actions. But if such truths can be shown to relate to the fulfilment of human nature, then they cannot be conceived as sets of unrelated moral propositions; they are intelligibly related to the nature of reality and of humanity.

However, to speak of an intended ideal is not yet to speak of fulfilment. For that, one has to grant the ideal some causal power over the universe, to say that the ideal purpose can be realized, so that pursuit of it is not vain. To commit oneself to the pursuit of love, as man's essential possibility, is to commit oneself to the faith that what is objectively intended can be actualized. The objective Idea of the Good which is mocked by a purposeless universe is a nightmare possibility, but one which renders moral effort wholly unintelligible, and thus undermines both the axiom of intelligibility and the necessity of moral commitment. To believe that what man essentially is, he can never be, is to disconnect morality from reason in a way which renders the saint the most pitifully schizophrenic of all men.

The saint, however, is a person who pursues a life of heroic self-renunciation because he believes that thereby he attains more nearly the true goal of humanity, because he believes that God commands him to do so, and because he hopes for a fulfilment in which God will share his own life with all those who turn to him in obedience. Only theism can unite these elements of intrinsic value, true humanity, absolute command and final fulfilment. Talk of intrinsic values alone, leaves morality disconnected from one's general view of reality and leaves their action-guiding force present indeed, but wavering and weak. Talk of Divine command alone makes morality sound like blind obedience to a powerful tyrant. Talk of essential humanity alone leaves one with the problem of what essential human nature is, and fails to provide adequate motive for pursuing it. And talk of final fulfilment alone ignores the categorical nature of moral obligation. The view of morality which theism licenses is of an absolute obligation to pursue intrinsic values which are constitutive of one's essential nature, and which are destined to lead to a final fulfilment of personal values, in relation to the supreme personal source and exemplar of all values.

There is a moral argument for theism, in so far as such a view of morality seems appropriate and adequate to one's own sense of moral obligation and responsibility, and in so far as one desires to relate one's moral outlook and practical commitments to a wider view of an intelligible universe, purposively created. The arguments from morality and intelligibility are mutually reinforcing; moral considerations require a modification of the necessitarian interpretation of intelligibility; and rational considerations require a modification of the Stoic commitment to moral action, whatever the universe is like. For it is only intelligible for a universe to contain moral freedom and categorical demands if there is an ultimate point in self-transcending moral commitment, a reason for moral striving which must lie in its achievement of a good which could be obtained in no other way. This is the good which Kant describes as 'happiness in accordance with virtue', a unique sort of self-creating through the giving of self to what is of intrinsic value. Without the possibility of that goal, the categorical demands of morality become impractical ideals. The fact that we deeply believe that they are not so, that we commit ourselves unreservedly to their implementation, expresses our practical commitment to the possibility of an intrinsically valuable goal in an intelligible universe, and to the existence of the God in whose almighty will and purpose such a goal can alone be grounded.

Moral commitment cannot be divorced from questions of rationality. The presupposition of taking morality to be a matter of absolute demands is that such objective demands have an intelligible placing in the scheme of things. Moral demands are not just commands, to be obeyed out of fear — this is what Kant called heteronomy. They have an irreducibly binding quality, an 'oughtness' which lays a claim upon one. When a theist talks of the will of God, he is not therefore grounding morality in some non-moral fact (of Divine command); he is identifying the nature of God as the objective foundation of irreducibly moral claims. Obligations are the temporal applications to specific circumstances of the eternal values which are rooted in the necessary being of God. Thus talk of absolute moral obligation requires both objective, necessary values and their application to changing human situations. The notion of a temporal God with an eternal nature, the creator of finite realities, fits the case perfectly. That is hardly surprising, for the notion of absolute obligations derives from a theistic background in the first place, and probably cannot long survive the dissolution of that background. But the argument is that we are certain in practice that there are such obligations, and if so, we are committed in practice to supposing the existence of an objective foundation for them which is very like God.

Not only is there an argument from the nature of moral demands; there is a similar argument from their content. Fundamental moral obligations cannot be contingently related to human possibilities; if they are rational, they must delineate a way of life which is possible for and proper to man; he must find his fulfilment in following them, even though they cannot be deduced from some prior notion of what human fulfilment is. One may say that an absolute command may hold out no hope of any future fulfilment; it is simply to be obeyed, whatever the consequences. But how, then, could one decide which apparent obligations were rational? Blind obedience is not a virtue; even if one must often neglect one's personal happiness, one should not neglect the question of human fulfilment in general. If obedience to absolute moral dictates will produce no foreseeable fulfilment for mankind in general, it becomes absurd. The obligatoriness remains. That cannot be undermined by any speculative argument; but it becomes a pointless and empty gesture in a tragic universe, like an arrow carefully aimed at nothing.

All the nobility of human life lies in moral striving and renunciation. In committing oneself to that, one is at least committing oneself to the hope that it will produce a sort of fulfilment which could be found in no other way. Morality requires not only a demand, but also a vision, a goal whose possibility makes its pursuit rational. One may place this vision in the far future, in some humanly attainable society, as Marxists do. Most religions, and certainly Christianity, take a darker view of human nature, and see that no fulfilment will be achieved while human nature remains as it is. To see at once the necessity and the impossibility of a morally just society and of a morally good life is to see the point at which morality is transcended and fulfilled by faith. It is transcended, not by simply giving up the struggle, and certainly not by a claim to have achieved perfection, but by an acceptance of failure combined with trust in a power beyond one's own which promises ultimate success. The ground for this trust is that the One who has made human nature can transform it, and by his action fulfil what we desire but are unable to achieve. The hope for heaven is not a hope for a reward for our moral efforts; it is the hope that what we unrelentingly attempt but always fail to achieve will be given on the sole condition of our acceptance of Divine grace.

To feel the tragic dimension of morality, in its absolute call to be perfected in love and our inescapable failure to respond to that call, is to begin to discover, not God himself, but the need for God. Just as, in the speculative realm, if there were a creator God, our desire for a total explanation of the world could in principle be met, so, in the moral realm, if there were a redeemer God, making possible by his own power what he demands, our desire for a categorical and rational morality could be met. The moral basis for theism lies in the absoluteness of moral requirements, their integral relation to human nature and its fulfilment, the ubiquitous sense of moral failure and the necessity of a Divine renewing power if any final moral purpose is to be realized in the universe. Only the concept of a God whose necessary nature defines what it is to be good, and whose active power aims always at what is good, can incorporate the tragic phenomenon of human morality into the vision of a rational and morally ordered universe, the existence of which makes possible sorts of value which could not otherwise exist. Again, there is no strict proof that the universe is such a place. But the complex commitments of the moral life may lead one to accept the hypothesis, not merely as rationally satisfying, but as supporting and enriching those practical commitments upon which one bases one's life. If this hope is vain, morality is absurd, though its compelling force remains. I believe that one should seek to avoid that conclusion, if it is possible to do so.

I have spoken of two senses in which God is good: he contains in himself, among his eternal ideas, the ideas of objective value which are the exemplary patterns of all goodness, and he always acts in ways which are good, in conforming to those patterns or realizing those values. The Thomist concept of God spoke of him as good in a rather different sense, as being himself the sum of all possible perfections, and thus as being supremeley desirable. Because of the arguments of chapter 3, I am unable to accept such a notion of metaphysical perfection. But that does not mean that one must give up any idea of God being the supreme ideal, supremely valuable in himself. We have considered God as a temporal agent, not only creating a world of free rational beings, but changing in response to them as well as guiding their development. If he can change, then he can, within the limits set by his immutable nature, change himself in accordance with any purposes he may have. We have seen that there exist certain basic values, such that, if a being chooses any values, he will have a good reason for choosing them. They are the values of power, knowledge, freedom, wisdom and happiness. It follows immediately that God will have a good reason for choosing such values for himself, and for choosing the maximal possible degree of each of them. Since there is nothing in his nature to prevent him doing so, and nothing external can limit God, it follows that God will be unsurpassably powerful, knowing, wise, free and happy.

One may, accordingly, speak of God as the uniquely perfect being, the being which possesses to the greatest possible degree all basic values, and which is necessarily unique in doing so. He will, of course, also possess many other values of all sorts, but it is hardly possible for us to conceive what God's nature is, except in the rather abstract, though very important, respects mentioned. No being could possibly be more perfect than God, for he is the necessary source of all possibility, and will choose for himself the highest possible values. To say that God is good is to say that he aims at the actualization of many possible values, both in himself and in any worlds he creates. The ultimate form of explanation for the world is that it is, as a whole, of intrinsic and unique value, and was so created as intentionally to express those values, which are necessarily rooted in the Divine being itself.

But does this mean that God, being good, must create

worlds expressing all the values that he can? No; it is not necessary that all valued states should actually exist. In fact, it is impossible for all possible values to co-exist, since they are often incompatible with each other. The value of sympathy, for example, could not exist in a world without failure or suffering. All that is necessary is that any world must actualize some set of values, that it must contain no evil which is not an implication of a value which is immeasurably greater than it and that it must be on the whole of unique and intrinsic value.

Even the being of God itself cannot contain all possible values. In so far as there are different sorts of value, not all commensurable with each other, not all capable of a maximal actualization, it will be senseless to speak of God as actualizing in himself the greatest degree of all possible values. Different sorts of beauty, for example, cannot be measured against each other so that one is the most beautiful possible thing, or that some set of beautiful things is the greatest possible actualization of beauty. Thus it will always be possible for God to possess more of some values, while possessing less of others. But one cannot say this would be absolutely better or worse, taken as a whole, even though one would then say that he was more perfect in some particular respect than he would otherwise have been.

The idea of a best possible world is incoherent, for any world could be better in some respect, and values cannot all be ranged on a scale with a clear maximal point. One must say that there is an infinite number of values of incommensurable sorts; some are greater or less than others, but there is often no objective standard of comparison — how does one compare the pleasure of a hot bath with that of hearing a symphony? So, of any world that God creates, it must be true that it is worth creating. But of no particular world is it true that it must exist, even in that sense of 'moral necessity' which, Leibniz thought, compelled a good God to create the best of all possible worlds.

God himself, being conceived as freely creative, could always have contained different particular values than he does, and more of some particular values than he does possess. God is not the best possible being, in the sense of having a logically maximal set of absolutely maximized properties; as with the best possible world, such a notion is incoherent. But he is the greatest conceivable being, in the intelligible sense that he alone possesses intrinsic values maximally. He is omnipotent and omniscient; his wisdom enables him to select ends of unique and complex value, and his power to effect the most efficient means to attaining them. So, though his wisdom could be exercised in different particular ways, it suffers from no defect the removal of which would make it greater than it is. Similarly, though there is no maximal degree of beatitude which could not logically be improved upon, God will necessarily possess the greatest actual degree of happiness at any time, a degree which flows from his uniquely great appreciation of all possible values. He will also possess an actual set of values which is necessarily greater than that of any other co-existing set, as well as being the source of all possible values. And, if he creates any world, his benevolence will extend to everything that exists, so that it will be uniquely unsurpassable, too. So, if there can be an ultimate rationale for the existence of any universe, it will be that this God freely chooses to express his eternal nature by communicating his goodness to creatures which he causes to exist by his own power, thereby also determining the specific forms of his goodness in creative ways.

Thus the world is explained as fully as possible by a twofold appeal: first, to the rational necessities which underlie the comprehensibility of all things, and, second, to the intrinsic values which give point to the existence of all things. God, the perfect being, unites in himself these two notions, and the polarities of necessity and contingency, moral freedom and reason, by freely choosing to bring into being a particular compossible set of values in one coherent universe.

In the pursuit of the moral life, man finds himself obligated to aim at values which hint at such an objective moral order. But, while the obligation is clear and insistent, the order is dimly and ambiguously seen. In such a universe, and only in such a universe, the values of faith, moral heroism and real self-determination can be exemplified. So, even in its times of despair, morality suggests the ground of faith and hope to which commitment testifies; but it never proves such a ground to one who desires to undertake neither commitment nor risk. The rational intelligibility which religion claims in its doctrine of God is no clear, calm, dispassionate lucidity. It is an obscure hint of an intelligibility which lies beyond full human comprehension, rooted in the doubts and agonies of a commitment to personal values in a universe of ignorance, pain and desire.

We may say, then, that the notion of a logically perfect being, creator of everything other than itself, is both coherent and is the foundation of the complete intelligibility and intrinsic value of the universe. As in scientific inquiry we commit ourselves to the rational comprehensibility of the world, so in moral commitment we stake our lives on the ultimate worthwhileness of the universe, an objective and realizable basis of value. But is the universe really intelligible and valuable? Even G. E. Moore, when he was a firm believer in objective value, thought that the universe, taken as a whole, was intrinsically evil. And in the light of all the irrationality, suffering and evil in the world, it may well be thought that to attribute such a world to a perfect creator verges on the absurd. Is theism a beautiful dream, an ultimately facile optimism, an escape from the realities of pain? Or can one suggest the ways in which a perfect creator might come to bring about such a world as this? It is perhaps on one's answer to that question, more than any other, that one's acceptance or rejection of theism, so far as it is rational, will depend.

9   The Existence of Evil

David Hume puts the argument in its most succinct and best-known form: 'Is God willing to prevent evil, but not able? Then is he impotent. Is he able, but not willing? Then is he malevolent. Is he both able and willing? Whence then is evil?' (*Dialogues Concerning Natural Religion*, pt. 10) Evil basically consists in the facts of pain, frustration and opposition, in all that obstructs or hinders or opposes human flourishing, or indeed the flourishing of all sentient creatures. The first and most obvious question to ask is whether a world is possible in which no such evil exists. It would be a world in which the desires and plans of sentient beings were never hindered or opposed. Whatever the answer to this question might be in the abstract, it seems clear that in any world at all like our own, such hindrance and opposition are an essential possibility.

Many of the things I want have to be worked for, and part of their attraction is that they take application and effort, persistence and resolution. People climb mountains not because they want to get to the top — they could always take a helicopter. They climb because of the challenge and the difficulty; because it is an achievement which brings out their last resources of strength and courage. Where the achievement of desires takes this form, it must always be possible to fail. One may be lazy or get discouraged; one may fail in strength or by aiming too high. There is always a risk, and the achievement is often more greatly valued where the risk of failure is greater. Men like to pit themselves against the elements, against their own resources of endurance and against each other; in this way most of the typically human pleasures are the products of difficult and uncertain striving. It is vital to see that the striving is not just externally related to the sort of pleasure that results; the pleasure is the sort of pleasure it is, because it is a striving, a conquest. And that inevitably involves much pain, in the form of defeat, failure and bad luck. So the first point one can make is that there are many sorts of happiness and worthwhile existence — and they include most of those available to humans — which entail the possibility and, indeed, the existence of a good deal of pain, discouragement and frustration.

This is true not only of many forms of happiness but of most forms of moral virtue. One could not have courage, for instance, if there were not obstacles to be overcome and fears to be faced; and where there are such things, there is always the possibility of defeat or danger. One could not have sympathy without disappointment with which to sympathize, or temperance without the possibility of over-indulgence and its consequences of ill-health, or justice without the possibility of partiality.

It also seems to be the case, and it has often been said, that men could not truly have freedom to choose their own courses of life or to mould their own futures within limits, if there was not the possibility of choosing a course which would impede the courses of others, and bring harm or suffering to them. If a creaturely and dependent will is given a measure of autonomy, then it may either look beyond its own being in freely chosen obedience to the will of the creator, or it may choose its own pleasure at the expense of others. It is true that a wise creature will see that he cannot finally be in control of his own life, that the choice of self is finally a hopeless one. Yet if he then chooses to obey God out of self-interest, his obedience will be selfishly motivated, and so will inevitably lead to just the consequences he wishes to avoid. Prudence offers no escape from the necessity of making a fundamental moral choice, which determines one's own destiny as well as affecting the lives of others for good or ill.

Why is such a moral choice, and the freedom it implies, of value? The traditional and, I think, the correct answer is that it is a condition of personal response, of unconstrained love, of being a person. God, of course, is not free in this way. It is not possible for God to experience in his own being the pleasures of difficult achievement, for nothing is difficult for God. Nor is it possible for him to overcome his own nature, for there is nothing to be overcome, nor for him to compete with other persons, for God has no equals or competitors. That means that he will lack all the sorts of values and acts and feelings which are distinctively human, but that is hardly surprising. God creates centres of awareness which may respond to him with either gratitude or resentment; and it is in that choice, confined to rational creatures, that freedom lies. Human persons add to the universe something which could not be in God — their own free striving, response and moral self-determining. The price of this is that they also add to the sorts of disvalue there are. While they can choose an everlasting life of growth in responsive love, they can also choose destruction and perhaps ultimate annihilation, for that is the consequence of rejecting the self-giving love upon which creation is founded.

Thus some dangers and evils are necessary conditions of the existence of the sorts of values that exist in this world. Some are possibilities of any world in which moral freedom exists, and are actualized when men choose evil over good (or, one might say, selfish and short-term good over general and long-term good). Many forms of natural evil, in the form of suffering, are necessary implications of the sort of universe of which we are part. The universe is such that from one or two simple general laws, increasingly complex patterns grow, producing new types of property which spring from and yet transcend the properties so far existent. At each stage of its temporal life, changes occur in accordance with principles of continuity, so that there are no unintelligible gaps or arbitrary discontinuities. Each new development builds upon what has gone before, while also adding something new. Thus chemistry is built upon the laws of physics, but observed chemical reactions are not reducible to those laws, considered on their own. And psychology is built upon similar laws, though it adds new principles of intentionality and awareness, with which physics does not deal. There are emergent properties, but all are continuously related to what has gone before, and do not 'break' or supersede the already established laws by which natural processes are shaped.

As well as this law-likeness, however, there also appear to be principles of randomness built into the structure of things. In quantum theory, one cannot say that every cause must necessarily produce a specific and determined effect. Rather, there are specifiable parameters within which a series of probability-states exist, realized as a result of statistical laws. Mechanism has given way to statistical probability; the once inviolable atoms disappear into patterns of energy-interchange, which can be mathematically quantified, but not uniquely determined, even in principle. In evolutionary theory, too, there is an acceptance of random mutation as a central part of the theory; so that chance plays a much greater part in the world than the rationalists wished to allow.

Of course, there is still much dispute about the interpretation of such theories, and many scientifically minded thinkers would still want to say that there are hidden variables which can explain the whole world mechanistically, that awareness is reducible to brain-states and that there is no quasi-purposive emergence at all, but only accidental survival or dissolution of organic material forms. But it is the case that belief in freedom and contingency requires the renunciation of determinism; thus an indeterministic theory, which allows events to be truly emergent, and so, from the point of view of lower levels of explanation, indeterminate, supports such a belief. On purely scientific grounds, the indeterminacy thesis holds the field; but it is a hypothesis which may well turn out to be false, in the form in which it is now held. What one must say, therefore, is that randomness within statistically probable parameters is just what is required to allow one both to maintain the rationality of nature and the existence of radical creativity within it. Such a view is metaphysically necessary to non-determinist theism. Fortunately, it seems that modern physics tends to support it.

The process which law and chance together govern is that of a continual emergence, an urge to development and self-unfolding, which works through conflict and striving, producing resolutions of tension which lead on to new tensions at higher emergent levels. Consciousness is only the most obvious of these supervening emergent qualities, which seem to show the development of an inner nisus towards the unfolding of sentient rational life. Each new substance finds itself at a specific point in this process, with a number of possibilities and limits. In accordance with its perception of its position, it strives more or less well to realize these possibilities and to develop them, and in doing so it both conflicts and co-operates with many other constantly developing substances. There is a constant striving to newness, to development. But such development allows many possible paths. One's desires can be channelled in many ways; one may seek to dominate others, or to submit to them or to pursue a harmonious inter-relation of a creative sort with them. Clearly, at the lower levels of nature, this is not a conscious process. The formation of patterns of order and conflict proceeds by unconscious entelechy, a process which appears from one end as a blind impulsive groping towards the unknown, and from the other as a drawing towards perfection by an Ideal archetype.

But what is it that is drawn? Classically, what has been envisaged is either a sort of *materia prima*, a pure potentiality, drawn into particularity by perfect Form, or a last outflowing of the perfect (thus Aristotle and Plotinus). But if one adopts a creationist view, perhaps the most helpful formulation is that of Leibniz. The primeval universe is the simplest possible positive entity, which is potential for the richest set of consequences, emerging by creative diversification, thereby obtaining 'as much variety as possible, but with the greatest order possible' (*Monadology*, 58). Allowing that there is no absolutely best possible world, one may say that this universe is essentially one which develops from a single initial configuration by creative choice towards the actualization of a set of ideal values the limits of which are set by the necessary nature of the Divine Ideal.

God, as efficient cause, posits the world, not as something arbitrarily made, but as a reality which is both his own polar opposite and also a projection of possibilities inherent but not actualizable in his own perfect being. The world is other than God, in that it is wholly dependent, conditioned by what is other than itself, whereas he is wholly self-determining; it develops largely by chance and unconscious process, whereas he is free, rational and fully aware; it is many, while he is one; and it is a place of conflict and striving, while he is one unified and unlimited will. Yet the world also expresses God, for it is in becoming other that the One expresses its real identity. Just as time is necessary to express the dynamism of God, which is an expression of his eternal nature, so otherness is necessary to express the love of God, which is a manifestation of his all-embracing unity. The Unchanging is endlessly expressed dynamically; the One is endlessly expressed in multiplicity, an infinity of self-images, mirroring the Indivisible in an infinite number of ways.

Thus God brings matter, as inert potency, into being, as the alien complement to his own active power. In giving birth to his opposite, he also manifests what he really is. The world is a projection into otherness of the Divine reality, a sort of negative image of God. Its destiny is to be drawn back into conscious unity with him, thereby realizing genuinely new values through the oppositions and conflicts inherent in such development. Out of the primeval state, plurality and spontaneity grow, and, as final cause and archetypal Ideal, God draws it in the direction of embodying his own perfection, by its own self-making.

At first, of course, there is no scope for conscious effort; unconscious randomness at the level of the atom and molecule is a condition for the flowering of freedom at the level of the higher organic forms, but is not itself a form of creative freedom. Slowly, there is drawn out from the primeval creation a set of partly random, partly spontaneously creative entities. God does not predetermine exactly what will be drawn. As creative ideal, he plays a continuous causal role in the development of the world, but this is more like a drawing or attracting than like an irresistible manipulation or a set of inscrutable interferences. God provides the initial natural laws of the universe, and its directional orientation, but he makes it such that a plurality of partially self-shaping substances can develop towards a free community of creative spirits. The Ideal of the world, that towards which it strives, is not a complete, wholly articulated form, leaving the universe without any contributory or creative role. Only the general features of the world are determined; its details fill in and develop gradually through time. Thus the world-process contributes to the reality of the Idea, in the process of embodying it in time. God himself participates in the creative advance of the world, as an increasing number of values come to be which could not exist in the one perfect being, originator of all, considered in isolation. One may even say that God can only realize many of the possibilities inherent in his own unlimited reality by going out from himself in loving and creative action to a form of otherness which, in turn, finds its true being only in a return to its undivided source.

The whole universe can be seen as the self-expressive act of God, and as justified in its being both by the new and unique sorts of value which its existence makes possible, and also by its ultimate transfiguration into a consciously achieved unity with its creative ground. Hegel, who has done more than any other philosopher to stress both the importance of the physical universe and its basis in Absolute Spirit, encapsulates this thought well when he writes, 'the Eternal Being manifests itself as the process of being self-identical in its otherness' (*The Phenomenology of Mind*, 7C, 775). But it must be stressed that otherness really is otherness, and not just an illusion. Finite creatures have real autonomy and individuality; they are not merely puppets in a Divine piece of cosmic self-indulgence. The Divine self-realization is precisely a self-relating, and therefore a vulnerability, to what is truly other than self. That God is the sole ground of this otherness does not undermine its given autonomy; and so the world essentially contains the possibilities of conflict, isolation and deceit which characterize personal relations. It must accordingly also contain, at sub-personal levels, the basic conditions which make alienated being possible.

The universe exists in order to bring into being a creative, contingent, free realization of purpose in a communal and evolving personal form of being, related to God as its source, ideal and guiding power. The sub-personal basis of contingent creativity is the factor of randomness, which eliminates determinism but at the same time eliminates absolute control. Where changes are partly random, there must be failures and imbalances as well as fortuitous and productive interactions. The sub-personal basis of rational purpose is the predictable law-likeness of being, which eliminates anarchy but also eliminates continuous providential adjustment of the laws. Where changes are law-governed, there must be particular cases in which general laws are disadvantageous or destructive as well as cases where they provide the basis for constructive planning. The sub-personal basis for a developing community of beings is a plurality of emergent forces, which eliminates monotony but also eliminates complete harmony. Where many individual substances each develop by interaction with each other, conflict and domination are as inevitable as cooperation.

Thus all those forms of natural evil which are involved in the factors of randomness, law-likeness, plurality and emergent striving can plausibly be seen as necessary conditions of having the sort of universe of which we are part. Now it is a logically clear and morally unexceptionable axiom that the existence of evil can be justified on the ground that it is a necessary implication of some otherwise unobtainable good, given, perhaps, that the good is overwhelmingly superior to the evil. God is not able to prevent those evils as long as he wills to achieve that good. If one continues to ask, 'But could an omnipotent creator not have arranged things otherwise?', one has missed the point. He could have created a different world, without us in it; but then the unique sorts of value which this world contains would not have existed; we would not have existed, as the persons we are. The only question is, will each creature receive an overwhelming and otherwise unobtainable sort of good from being part of such a world as this? If the answer is 'Yes', then, however difficult it may be to face evil in practice, the creation of such a world by a perfect God will be intelligible.

What one has to do, in order to show how a perfect God could create this world, is to show that the evil in it is a necessary implication of the good, and that the good is unique and overwhelmingly greater than the evil. One must also add that the evil of one creature cannot be balanced by the good of another. There is a sense in which each sentient individual, having a consciousness which cannot be shared, is a separate universe. And God cannot aggregate an evil universe and a good one to produce a state good on the whole. Each universe must contain more good than evil; thus God can only create a world in which every sentient being has an overwhelming good possible to it. This does not at all imply that each individual will have the same amount of good, and certainly not that each will have the same sort of good. There may be a rich and complex universe in which an infinite number of beings have greatly differing amounts and sorts of good; all the existence of a perfect God requires is that each will have the possibility of a realization of overwhelming good in itself.

Another thing that one may wish to add is that a perfect creator must be conceived as himself sharing in the pain and suffering of the universe, if not in its moral evil. When David Hume presents his stark vision of an amoral universe, he writes, 'The whole presents nothing but the idea of a blind nature, impregnated by a great vivifying principle, and pouring forth from her lap, without discernment or parental care, her maimed and abortive children' (*Dialogues,* pt. 11). Nature is blind, without discernment or care. But if one sees the origin of created being in an omniscient God, then care and discernment are involved in creation in two ways. First, God is concerned that his purpose should be realized; that purpose, rooted in his own immutable nature, is to achieve the fulfilment of personal being, in delight, creativity and community. Second, God has a full and intimate knowledge of all his creatures, and though we have no idea what the Divine knowledge is like, it must include a sympathetic appreciation of the pains and enjoyments of sentient creatures.

God must directly know all that we feel. It is quite unsatisfactory to conceive his knowledge as a sort of purely mathematical or propositional knowledge, as if by a detached and passionless observer, as if God was the great computer, affected by nothing, but storing all data. God's knowledge must be conceived as being fully personal, and that means that it must be involved; it must have affective and reactive tone, must involve an inward response in his own being. To know a personal reality is more than to register neutrally that it exists; it is to enter in some way into its reality, in a reactive response in which evaluation, feeling and judgement are closely interwoven. So one must conceive God as taking delight in the happiness of his creatures, and as being pained at their sufferings.

If one speaks of God 'including' all experiences, this is a

metaphorical usage, and must not undermine the essential autonomy of the created self. Human experience is essentially bound up with human action, and in all experiencing there is an element of subjectively contributed assessment and interpretation. Because of that, it is not possible for one personal being literally to possess another person's experience, without becoming that other person. God cannot have my suffering, but, in fully apprehending it, his own being is changed by active sympathy. Our suffering causes him to suffer, in a way which the greatest human sympathy only dimly mirrors. One must say that the possibility of suffering is rooted in the necessary being of God, that it is actualized in him, as it is in different ways in creation, and that in him it is transfigured by that greater beatitude which arises from wider knowledge of the overwhelming value of created existence.

The classical conception of an impassible God, who is unchanged by the sufferings of the world, is totally inadequate as an interpretation of perfection. If love is a perfection, then a form of suffering-with creatures must be an essential moment of the Divine life, which qualifies the nature of his supreme beatitude. God, as perfect, must remain a being of unsurpassable bliss. But it is a happiness which includes, transforms and overcomes suffering and sorrow, which, in that sorrow, expresses an inherent quality of its own being and which thereby is able to have a moral grandeur and depth unknown to more innocent pleasure.

Pain is something that every rational being would seek to avoid. Yet its existence is involved in sentience, and it is mixed with pleasure in subtle ways, so that its absence would make the world incalculably different. The tragic quality of our world is that it is a place where love is constantly defeated, and yet most fully and uniquely expressed in its defeat. Such a world is, in the proper sense, terrible, but it contains glories that could exist in no other world. Perhaps we would not like to have to decide whether or not such a world should be. We might admit its grandeur, its magnificence, its agonized nobility of spirit, yet we might not dare to admit it into existence, this goodness bought at the cost of such appalling cruelty.

God could have created instantaneously a sensuous paradise for all creatures, as the early Genesis myth supposed he did. But the denizens of that world would have been radically unlike humans, who carry their animal inheritance about with them until they die. We are creatures which have emerged by conflict, effort, aggression and random mutation, within a world which develops according to the simplest principles by statistical probability to a complex and many-levelled universe. We are what we are because of our past, part of a long evolutionary process, partly accidental products of a vast cosmos whose final design is as yet beyond our comprehension. Mankind as we know it is one small part of this universal striving to goals perhaps indefinitely distant. He is not, and never was, a pampered child in a privileged garden; he is the development of a million mutations and genetic recombinations.

Once one has such a broad vision of cosmic evolution — a vision impossible equally to Hume and to Aquinas — it is not at all clear that nature presents itself as a blind, uncaring process. It is true that it scarcely presents itself as the work of the sort of loving Father who is concerned to protect his erring children from all harm, keeping them in a state of infantile dependence. I should have thought that a more natural picture is of a purposive process, oriented to the realization of values which essentially involve conflict and suffering. Such a process does seem indifferent to the fate of many individuals; it remains enigmatic in its structure and final goals, and also shows signs of the presence of destructive or demonic powers of evil, as well as a general orientation to the good. These puzzling factors must all be taken account of, in any attempt to construe the relation of God and the world. When people say that there is no solution to the problem of evil, they usually mean that there is no unambiguous and definitively established account of these factors, or that there is no way available to us of showing the truth of such an account. That there could be a solution — that is, that the world could be intelligibly derived from a perfect God — is fairly clear. I would go further, and suggest that in suffering itself one can find a sense of Divine presence and sympathy which, in shattering one's self-reliance, leads one to discover a quality of absolute trust in a goodness which is beyond all change. It is in darkness that one turns to light, to trust in the God who kills and brings to life, who creates both darkness and light, who in the depth of his own being suffers and overcomes and calls us to share his life in hope.

I am not suggesting the absurd position that one can infer directly from evil to God. Rather, the world suggests a rational and morally purposive ground clearly enough for evil to present itself as a problem, not merely as an unpleasantness. And the experience of suffering, while it can be crippling and destructive, can also be a means through which faith is purified, courage forged and hope generated. It can be a means of giving one deeper insight into the nature of God, as suffering and redeeming love. It can therefore be seen as itself part of the purpose of this creation, of this painful process of self-making which issues in the final transfiguration of self-abandoning love.

If there is no possibility of final transfiguration, any such talk can be no more than a self-deluding sham. If it is necessary that each sentient being must have the possibility of achieving an overwhelming good, then it is clear that there must be some form of life after earthly death. Despite the many pointers to the existence of God, theism would be falsified if physical death was the end, for then there could be no justification for the existence of this world. However, if one supposes that every sentient being has an endless existence, which offers the prospect of supreme happiness, it is surely true that the sorrows and troubles of this life will seem very small by comparison. Immortality, for animals as well as humans, is a necessary condition of any acceptable theodicy; that necessity, together with all the other arguments for God, is one of the main reasons for believing in immortality.

There is an evident tension between the importance I have ascribed to rational freedom, the basic autonomous ability to choose either good or evil, and the necessity that each sentient being should receive an overwhelming and unique good in its own total existence. For it seems that if a free being does finally choose evil, no such overwhelming good can come to it. This fact, however, requires only a slight qualification to what I have said: namely, that it must always be *possible* for each being to achieve such a good. If it does not, it must be by reason of its own choice. Moreover, ultimately, evil must be eliminated from each community of moral beings, either by all who have chosen evil eventually coming to see the emptiness and uselessness of their choice and so repenting, or, if their choice has somehow become irrevocable, by their annihilation or total exclusion from the community. In the end, any remaining evil must be of the agent's own choice, and the loss of the possible overwhelming good must be entirely his responsibility. Only on such a principle can any doctrine of hell be rendered compatible with the existence of a perfect creator of all things.

It is a measure of the ignorance and ambiguity of human existence that one cannot obtain knowledge of any such life after death. This life remains a pilgrimage in darkness; the existence of God, immortality and even human freedom itself, cannot be unambiguously established. Why should this be so? Kant suggested that such ignorance or ambiguity was necessary if genuine moral commitments were to be possible, as opposed to calculations of prudent self-interest. For, though moral commitment carries with it the hope for fulfilment, it is the commitment which gives rise to the hope, and not vice versa. We might extend that argument a little, and say that ignorance is a condition of trust, of learning, of independence and of solitude. It is not, after all, that we have no knowledge of God; rather, that knowledge is inconstant, dim and rather abstract. It requires constant re-affirmation, and the disposition to see one's experience as a realm of moral challenges, disclosures of meaning and value, intimations of an underlying personal presence and objective purpose.

Early Christian theology, with its lack of any evolutionary ideas, was forced to see our present situation as a fall from previous perfection. The Fathers postulated that Adam, the first man, possessed the Divine gifts of sonship (a direct knowledge of God's presence and will) and natural justice (the ability to control one's impulses always and easily). This must seem a very unrealistic view to anyone who accepts some form of evolutionary theory and accepts that much evil is an inevitable consequence of such a world. It seems to reflect the tendency to place a morally ideal situation at some point in the past, in a Golden Age now lost. And it forces an almost totally negative evaluation of work, suffering and death, as results of a morally culpable disobedience. Of course, whether or not Adam existed is wholly irrelevant to the problems now facing mankind; it is only important as part of a theodicy, to explain why death and suffering now exist.

That theodicy is quite unsatisfactory. Death and suffering are natural and necessary parts of the evolutionary process, and it is irrational to feel guilt for what is inevitable. A more positive view can be taken of these factors, as making possible a growth to full personhood and moral sonship from a condition of animal amorality, by way of a slow and difficult disentanglement from ignorance and desire. To quote Hegel again: 'Otherness itself, i.e. cancelling and superseding its own pure thought-constituted notion, lies in the very notion of Spirit' (*The Phenomenology of Mind*, 7C, 769). He sees Absolute Spirit as becoming alienated from itself, so that nature is 'the untrue existence of Spirit', and then returning to itself again in a form of conscious knowledge which is only possible because of the alienation: 'Spirit in its entirety . . . is once more the process from its immediacy to the attainment of a knowledge of what it implicitly or immediately is; and is the process of attaining the state where the shape and form, in which it appears as an object for its own consciousness, will be perfectly adequate to its essential nature, and where it will behold itself as it is' (ibid., 690).

A fully theistic interpretation of Hegel will want to deny that the universe is simply the process of Absolute Spirit objectifying itself and returning back into itself. The perfect being does remain transcendent to the universe, even though finding a unique form of self-expression in relating itself to a created world. Yet the notion of solitude, autonomy and independence are integrally involved in the idea of a 'truly other' creation, and the relation of that other to God must take the form both of a fulfilment and of a cancellation of its being. The relation is a fulfilment, because only thereby will it discover its real basis and purpose; and a cancellation, because only by free self-giving can it find what it truly is.

The human world is ambiguous and framed by paradox, because it essentially expresses the polarities, implicit in the Divine being itself, of identity and otherness, sharing and solitude, self-fulfilment and self-denial. God, from the fulness of his everlasting being, gives himself to what he draws from nothing. Man, in his emptiness and precarious existence, absurdly seeks to cling to what he cannot control. To find the right balance in this tremulous but necessary relationship, to find a form of authentic self-determination which is also a freely chosen obedience, which attains a freedom beyond the rage which destroys and the fear which submits, is a task which is likely to be long and difficult. It requires a world in which man is free to work out to the end the consequences of his own desires, and discover for himself the way to the fulness of vision he needs. In some such way as this one might suggest that human nature and destiny remain enigmatic, for a fuller knowledge would destroy entirely the nature of the spiritual quest which can alone lead to the fruition of the Divine purpose for human life. Mystery and paradox make possible the spiritual quest upon which mankind is engaged; we have hints and promptings to make the quest seem intelligible, but it is we who must prepare ourselves so that we may become ready to receive a knowledge which, fully given, might now destroy us, as autonomous and morally free beings.

Nevertheless, though much evil is necessary, the very fact that we are morally free entails that not all of it is. It is impossibly idealistic to suppose that we could be, or ever could have been, able perfectly to control our natural impulses of lust and aggression, so deeply engrained by evolution. Yet it is quite clear that there is much culpable evil in the world, and few would claim to be free of guilt. Moreover, there do seem to be forces of destruction and evil which seize upon human weakness to produce terrifying but apparently unavoidable catastrophes like the great World Wars. Here the early Christian myth of Satan as a fallen spiritual being, though not very biblical, appeals to the thought that this world may be only part of a much wider cosmic drama, in which forces of good and evil battle for supremacy.

The developed idea of Satan probably originated in the dualistic cosmogeny of Zoroastrianism. A theist who believes in the creation of the world by a perfect being cannot suppose that an independent power of evil exists, uncreated by God. Nor can he suppose that God wills evil. The only possibility is that the source of avoidable evil lies in a being dependent upon God, but possessing moral autonomy. God cannot eliminate evil without eliminating the beings who freely choose it, and though evil is to be absolutely opposed, God permits it because he will bring from it a unique sort of good, the good of the one saved from destruction.

It is a perfectly coherent supposition that there are spiritual beings of great power who have chosen evil, and who involve this world in the anarchy and distortion of their struggles to accept or reject the powers of love. So it may seem that the world into which we are born is one in which there is some inevitable evil, born of its evolutionary character. In this world human society is corrupted by the past evil choices of our ancestors, spiritual powers of destruction as well as beneficent powers for good are at work and the human will is consequently predisposed by its own weakness to compound the evil. Yet in all this, God, as the hidden source and goal of all being, persistently and endlessly draws all things towards the final fulfilment of their proper natures, a consummation of overwhelming value which includes and transfigures all the evil whose possibility is necessarily implied in the creation of this world, and whose actuality has largely resulted from the free choices of creatures.

Just as early religious myths were largely speculative attempts to account for the perceived enigmas of good and evil, the contrast of clear signs of purpose and moral demand with the ruthless destructiveness and profligacy of nature, so these suggestions are speculative hints towards showing how the evil of the world can be a necessary implication of the distinctive and overwhelming sorts of good that it will realize. Man is drawn from darkness and ignorance, thrown into a moral battleground between forces beyond his comprehension, and destined to begin an endless journey towards the light, after he has played his own part in this arena. The details of my account may be wrong. But some such account is coherent. And some such account must be true, if theism is true. It is consistent with the account itself that it must be committed belief in God which leads one to hope for everlasting life; that hope never becomes knowledge in this life, and its outlines can only be dimly sketched, by guesswork and desire.

It may be thought that I have sought to prove too much, that this account makes the existence of a loving God unfalsifiable, since no amount of evil would contradict it. But it is quite simply true that no amount of evil will contradict the existence of a perfect God, as long as the requirement is met, that it is necessarily implied in the existence of a world which leads to overwhelming good. It is the existence of that good which is falsifiable, in principle. But it can never be falsified in this world, for the sort of good in question requires the co-existence of suffering and ignorance now.

There is a danger in this view. That is, that it justifies evil too much, making it an essential part of God's will, and therefore not finally opposable. Hegel comes near the justification of evil as good, when he writes, 'Evil is nothing else than the self-concentration of the natural existence of Spirit . . . it really constitutes the essential moment of the self of Spirit' (*The Phenomenology of Mind*, 773, 775). The danger in such expressions is that they may be used as justifications for policies of oppression and force. It must therefore be clearly seen that evil is never an end or a means to an end; it is never something that should be chosen. It is inevitably implied in the existence of the sort of world we have, but it should never be said that God chooses the evil. He chooses the good, and accepts evil as its necessary concomitant; but that evil should always be opposed and eliminated, so far as is possible. Indeed, if suffering has any positive part to play in God's plan at all, it is as something to be resisted and overcome. Some evil may be inevitable; but any evil which can be eliminated by human action should be.

It is also wrong to think that, if a man can remove some suffering, then God could have done so, and thus should have done so. If creatures are given autonomous powers, then the world in which they act must be one which both sets limits to those powers and is shapeable by them. If a particular creature is free to cause harm or refrain from doing so, God can neither force him to refrain nor prevent the harm himself, except by removing that creaturely freedom. So, if a creature is free, by research and effort, to remove some suffering, God cannot remove it himself without undermining the whole structure of human freedom. So it is quite unrealistic to suppose that God could have removed all disease, and at the same time sustain the sort of universe in which conflict, effort and freedom are integral factors.

What could perhaps be true, consistently with human freedom and the general evolutionary character of the cosmos, is that God could guide, sustain and inspire the efforts of creatures to overcome the negative results of conflict, and that he could act to heal and save from harm on occasions and to an extent that does not undermine the general structure of reality. There might be providential Divine guidance, and particular 'miraculous' salvific acts, which would not undermine the structure of law and human autonomy, but might point to a fulfilment of that structure and autonomy in a wider context of relation to the Divine.

We can have little or no idea of the scope and limits of such Divine action. But one might be fairly confident that a temporal and loving God will interact positively with his creation, in ways which never contradict its structure, but which point to its final value and fulfilment. God is at every stage the Ideal which draws on the present towards a future which more fully reflects the Divine nature, and at every stage, he responds to the universe by including its reality in his ever-growing knowledge. Thus far, Whitehead's 'philosophy of organism' provides one with an idea of God which is far superior to the Thomist notion. God is a dipolar being; as primordial, 'he is the unlimited conceptual realisation of the absolute wealth of potentiality' (*Process and Reality*, p. 521) and the Place of Forms; as consequential, he is the constantly developing transmutation of many temporal actualities into one all-embracing experience, the knower and lover of all things. Yet Whitehead's God does not truly interact with the world; he includes it, and provides the source of its possible futures and the reservoir of its completed experiences. But any creating is done by the many actual occasions which constitute the process of reality; the cosmic tyrant, against whom Whitehead so strongly protests, has become the cosmic sponge, absorbing all experiences, but contributing nothing except an abstract array of eternal possibilities for the creative multiplicity of the world.

Those theologians who protest against process theology often do so because of a sense that God has been rendered powerless. They feel he has become a spectator of the world he includes, himself part of a creative process he cannot control, wedged helplessly between creativity, 'the ultimate metaphysical ground', and the countless actual occasions which project the world into the future. There is some justice in this charge. We do not want God to be a monarchical tyrant, determining by his omnipotent will everything that happens, and we do not want him to be the remote designer of 'the machine of the universe', leaving it to its own concerns. On the other hand we do not want him to be the helpless experient of all its feelings, a 'fellow-sufferer' who never himself appears to act. The finite world must be given the sort of autonomy and importance Whitehead wants, but God must be related to it more positively than he seems to allow. God must not only act; he must ultimately control the universe fully, guiding it to its unique and proper fulfilment, in finally conscious relation to himself.

If this is so, one might hope to see signs of his guidance and foreshadowings of that fulfilment. One might not expect to be able sharply to distinguish between the work of nature, man and God. God must normally work within the continuities of nature which he has established, but they allow many possibilities of directing, shaping or modifying. The theist will tend to find Divine action in events which seem to reverse evil or to 'answer' prayer, especially in creative or courageous actions of sentient beings. One can never say unequivocally what is of God, or how the Divine causality is refracted through the fields of social and personal life, with all its ambiguities and tensions. But, in general, one may see God as continually forming the pattern of the developing world, and rational creatures as generating in response a communal and largely self-generated image of his perfect and uncreated life. Rational theology cannot say what God may have revealed of himself and his purposes. But it can certainly lead up to the point of making it wholly intelligible that such a being might reveal to men the mystery of his action in the world, and confirm the ambiguous signs of his purpose in some distinctive way. At that point, however, the task of natural theology ends in its final realization that the long, hard search for the Divine has all the time been guided by the prior action of the One whose self-showing continually draws humanity towards himself.

10   The Idea of Infinity

In this final chapter, I want to locate the idea of God which I have outlined within the historical development of philosophical theism. In this way, I hope to make clear how it can claim to be a traditional concept, while differing in many ways from particular views which are sometimes, rather narrowly, taken to represent the whole tradition.

The history of philosophy, Whitehead suggested, is a series of footnotes to Plato. Though he could hardly be said to have left a systematic rational theology, Plato did define the intellectual terms in which rational theism has ever since been developed in the West. His best-known and most fundamental distinction was between the changeless world of *Eide*, the Forms which provide the only true knowledge of reality, and the changing, half-real world of sense-perceived material things. Set mysteriously at the apex of the Forms is what Plato calls 'a thing that every soul pursues as the end of all her actions, dimly divining its existence, but perplexed and unable to grasp its nature' (*Republic*, 505). Of it, he writes, 'the highest object of knowledge is the essential nature of the Good, from which everything that is good and right derives its value' (ibid., 504). The Good is 'beyond being, surpassing it in dignity and power' (ibid., 508). But Plato refuses to say more of it, the ultimate cause and object of intellectual knowledge. Here is a first but unmistakable adumbration of the God of the philosophers. But its relation to the other Forms and to matter, which is apparently independently existent, is left wholly obscure. To account for the nature of the material universe, Plato introduces a Demiurge, who uses the Forms in shaping matter as well as he can. But where he comes from, or why he should have the nature he does, is again left tantalizingly without explanation. So, at the beginning of Western philosophy, one has a hint, or an obscure sketch, of the doctrine that material reality has a conceptual basis, and that the truly real is the changeless, the good and the immaterial, hidden from the senses but knowable by the disciplined intellect. This is a form of theism, albeit one calclated to appeal only to intellectuals or ascetics. It is a vision of reality from which few theistic philosophers have been able to free themselves completely, whether they would describe themselves as Platonists or not.

It was Aristotle, however, who was to be the philosophical mentor of later Christian theology. In *Metaphysics* Λ, he develops the idea of an eternal and immovable substance, whose very essence must be to act, to move the outer sphere of the fixed stars. In fact, every heavenly sphere requires its own unmoved mover, so that 'there must be as many such substances as there are motions of the stars' — which he variously estimates to be either 47 or 55. There is, however, one prime unmoved mover, and it is best conceived as an intelligence. This intelligence will live a life 'such as the noblest and happiest that we can live', that is, it will always be engaged in contemplative thought. Since it must changelessly think of what is best, and since the best possible thing is the Divine intellect itself, its object of thought must be itself. It is, says Aristotle in a famous phrase, *noesis noeseos,* 'a thinking of thinking'. 'The object of thought and the act of thinking do not differ in the case of immaterial things.' The intellect receives into itself the Form of the object it thinks about, and knower and known are one in the moment of knowledge. Whatever the obscure process of thought by which Aristotle arrives at these conclusions, he does propound a doctrine of God as 'a living being, eternal and most good; to him belong — or rather, he is — life and duration, continuous and eternal'. God, the prime mover, is so self-sufficient that he depends on nothing other than himself in any respect. So, whatever it knows, it must know by inspection of itself alone. Its activity, being purely intellectual, is changeless, and consists in the contemplation of its own essence. And since, for Aristotle, knowing is a sort of actual uniting with the Form of its object, if God knows himself, then his knowledge and its objects, being pure Forms, are one.

It may seem that such a changeless self-contemplator can hardly be the efficient cause of the world. And indeed, like Plato, Aristotle regards matter as ungenerated. How, then, is it caused to move by the prime mover and all the subordinate unmoved movers? Here, he suggests that perhaps 'the final cause moves by being loved, while all other things that move do so by being moved'. The outer sphere of the fixed stars is moved into an eternal circular motion by its love of the perfection of the prime mover, who loves and contemplates himself changelessly, because of his own perfection.

It is well known that Aristotle rejected the Platonic theory of an independently existing world of Forms, and insisted that Forms, though real, were to be found only embodied in things. But, in his doctrine of God, he does seem to have the conception of an existent pure Form, which is the sum of all possible perfections. It was a very small step from here to Augustine's doctrine that all Forms were existent, not in some independent realm of their own, but in the mind of God. However, Aristotle's conception of the relation of God to the world is obscure. The eternal existence of matter seems to compromise the search for intelligible explanation which led him to formulate the famous arguments for the existence of a prime mover; for it remains forever beyond rational explanation. And how matter can have love for the prime mover, without itself being conscious, is incomprehensible. Perhaps he has in mind some sort of unconscious attraction, or nisus towards the perfect, as though the universe is drawn from nothing towards a finally unattainable perfection, just by the attracting power of the changelessly perfect

— which all the time remains unaware of the striving of matter to imitate it.

Thus in Aristotle, Plato's notion of the Good is characterized as 'a living being', the Divine Intellect in which all Forms have their place, as objects of the Divine contemplation and at the same time as identical with the Divine essence. This conception is, I think, an essential element in any rational theism, and it provides the basis for the existence of eternal truths of reason and morality and of those changeless possibles which set the necessary limits of the Divine activity. But the idea of Divine activity is severely limited by the Aristotelian account. It can only consist in self-contemplation, and the form of causality it exercises upon the world can only be that of final causality — being the goal towards which the world unconsciously moves. In this respect, Aristotle is the progenitor of the interpretation of the Divine infinity as exclusive. God is unlimited, in excluding everything finite or limited; his being has nothing in common with the being of the world; he does not originate or actively modify it. Its existence is not caused by him in any active way; and its greatest efforts to achieve likeness to the self-sufficient *noesis noeseos* are doomed to failure, by the very nature of matter. Happiness and perfection are for the gods, not for humans.

It is, perhaps, surprising that this doctrine is the one that was baptized into Christian orthodoxy, most notably by Thomas Aquinas. Partly, no doubt, it was because of the immense authority which the newly discovered works of Aristotle, coming through the Arabian commentators, had achieved. Aristotle's metaphysical arguments from intelligibility to an immutable, eternal prime mover put in classical form the process of thought which still underlies the rational justification of theism. And his statement of the changeless perfection of the Divine Being seems, at least at first, admirably to meet the demands of worship. The Christian sometimes feels that he is but dust and ashes before a totally other holiness and perfection, with which he can have nothing in common. He sometimes feels the need for a changeless stillness, far removed from the failures and corruptions of the world. It is no accident that the ideal of contemplative stillness, untainted by the world, has always been part of the Christian tradition. The exclusively infinite God of Aristotle, unmoved by anything that happens in the sublunary realm, untouched by time or passion, expresses and enshrines that ideal. To contemplate the Divine, to share the Beatific vision to some degree, is the greatest desire of all who are ultimately moved by love for the final cause.

Yet the Christian God, as portrayed in the Bible, is a God who creates the world, who constantly changes in his reaction to his creatures, choosing and rejecting them in accordance with their responses to him, and even, eventually, suffering and dying as man, in Jesus Christ. How can the immutable and impassible being create and redeem the world through his own love? How can he answer prayer, grieve for sin and rejoice in salvation? The problem is so great that the God of popular Christianity has sometimes been quite a different being from the God of the theologians and philosophers. The trouble is that he has sometimes been an anthropomorphic, petty and rather obnoxious 'person in the sky'. The flight from the passionless God of theology produces a naive and superstitious fantasy-figure, quite unworthy of the attention, let alone the worship, of rational beings. Despite Pascal's vision of fire, we do not want to return to the 'God of Abraham, Isaac and Jacob' if the price is the rejection of reason and morality.

Aquinas was well aware of the problem, and devoted many subtle volumes to the attempt to reconcile an exclusively infinite God with the doctrines of creation and redemption. I have argued that this attempt is doomed to failure. A self-sufficient being can give no rationale for creation, and a necessary being cannot give rise to a world of contingent, free creatures. Yet the Thomist doctrine is not simply to be rejected. It is quite correct in ascribing to God the metaphysical perfections of aseity, necessity, unity, immutability and completeness. These are the presuppositions of the intelligibility of the world. Its basic error is in supposing that God is logically simple — simple not just in the sense that his being is indivisible, but in the much stronger sense that what is true of any part of God is true of the whole. It is quite coherent, however, to suppose that God, while indivisible, is internally complex. In particular, he may be necessary and immutable in some respects, but not in others. Thus the Divine nature and existence will be necessary; God could not fail to exist, as a being possessing the basic metaphysical and personal perfections that he does possess. The nature of God is such that, if it is possible, then it is actual. It follows that the nature of God, in these respects, is immutable; it cannot be changed, destroyed or modified, either by itself or by another. We might say, further, that at least a vast number of possibilities and values (the Forms) are similarly necessary and immutable, being constitutive of the essence of the Divine Being. God is necessarily omnipotent and omniscient (knowing and being able to do anything logically possible); he is happy, wise and good (realizing the greatest actual set of values in himself, without error or imperfection).

So far, the Thomist conception of God is illuminating and satisfactory. But the mention of these latter perfections, those which I called the personal perfections of God, since they imply the presence of consciousness in some form, begins to raise difficulties. How can a being which is necessary and immutable have the power to do everything? Being necessary, it cannot do anything other than it does. Being immutable, it cannot do anything new or original. For Aristotle, this was no problem, since God only contemplates himself in one changeless activity. Even so, are there not many things such a God cannot do? Could he create a world of free creatures, for example, or do something he has never done before? The obvious reply is to say that God does everything logically possible for him to do; there is nothing he could do which he does not do. Thomas's God, however, has to create the universe *ex nihilo*; he has to bring it into being by a free act of choice among possibles. This hypothesis improves on the unintelligibility of matter in the Aristotelian system, for it ascribes matter wholly to the creative act of God, instead of leaving it as an inexplicable surd. But it does seem to relate God to a reality outside himself, and so to compromise his self-sufficiency. Is it possible, just as one can speak of a changeless Divine act of self-contemplation, to speak of a changeless Divine act of creation? The whole universe will issue from God by a changeless decree; creation will cause no change in God, and time and change will be ultimately unreal aspects of how the universe is seen by finite creatures within it.

But even if creation can be seen as a timeless Divine act, the real difficulty remains, that, since the being of God is wholly necessary, it will be a necessary act, which could not have been otherwise in any respect. This view is still in tension with a central strand of the Christian tradition: namely, that God need not have created any universe, and that he need not have created precisely this universe. How can a necessary being be free in any way?

The rationalist answer to this question is that God is free in that he is self-determined, or not sufficiently caused by another. It is Leibniz who states the view in its most succinct form. The universe is not metaphysically necessary, because its essence does not involve its existence. But it is 'determined in such a way that its contrary would imply imperfection or moral absurdity' (*On the Ultimate Origin of Things*). God sees all possible worlds, in his own being, and he chooses to bring into being that which is best, in accordance with the principle of perfection. Since God is perfect, he cannot do other than bring into being the best of all possible worlds. Thomas had already denied the view that there can be such a thing as 'the best possible world', so he could not put the doctrine in that way. Yet it was open to him to say that, since God is good, and since the existence of a universe containing an overwhelming number of good things is good, God must by necessity of his nature, choose to create some universe. His choice is changeless, but one might say that there were alternatives to it, in the sense that other worlds are logically possible.

Two things, however, prevented Thomas from putting the point quite like that. First, there was the Christian dogma that God did not have to create any world at all. And second, that it is odd to speak of a choice between alternative worlds when God cannot do other than he does. So, although both these views seem to offer satisfactory developments of the Greek doctrines of God, they both founder on the rock of creation. Leibniz's God creates a wholly necessitarian universe, but it must be doubted whether the idea of a logically best possible world is a coherent conception. Thomas's God changelessly creates one out of many possible worlds, but it seems that his choice must be conceived both as a choice between alternatives and as unable to be other than it is, at the same time. This antinomy between freedom and necessity signals the final wreck of the doctrine of exclusive infinity. The infinite God, who is complete in himself without the world, and who is necessarily and immutably what he is, cannot bring into being a finite universe by creation (by free choice) without some determining modification of his own being, and that contradicts the hypothesis.

The obvious alternative is to say that the world does not originate by free choice, but flows from the Divine being by necessity. Then, however, one cannot define God as self-sufficient without any world, for some world, and indeed this precise world, is necessary to his being what he is. For a complete specification of the nature of the self-sufficient being, one has to include the world as well. The notion of Divine infinity accordingly changes to that of inclusive infinity, a reality which is unlimited precisely because there is nothing it excludes; it includes everything limited within itself. As Hegel